MICA's 11th International Communication Management Conference
(MICA ICMC 2025)

Marketing in the Digital Age: Navigating Disruptions and Embracing Innovations

(Book of Abstracts)

Editors

Dr. Varsha Jain
Dr. Amit Karamchandani

ICMC 2025

MICA
THE SCHOOL OF IDEAS

ALLIED PUBLISHERS PVT. LTD.

Noida • Mumbai • Kolkata • Chennai • Bangalore

ALLIED PUBLISHERS PRIVATE LIMITED

D-5, Sector-2, **Noida**–201 301
Ph. Nos.: 0120-4320295/2542557/4352866 • E-mail: delhi.books@alliedpublishers.com

17 Chittaranjan Avenue, **Kolkata**–700072
Ph.: 033-22129618 • E-mail: cal.books@alliedpublishers.com

15 J.N. Heredia Marg, Ballard Estate, **Mumbai**–400001
Ph.: 022-42126969 • E-mail: mumbai.books@alliedpublishers.com

No. 25/10, Commander-in-Chief Road, Ethiraj Lane (Next to Post Office)
Egmore, **Chennai**–600008
Ph.: 044-28223938 • E-mail: chennai.books@alliedpublishers.com

P.B. No. 9932, No. 15, 3rd Floor (Next to Vijaya Bank), 5th Cross, Gandhinagar,
Karnataka, **Bangalore**–560009, Ph.: 080-41530285 / 22386239
E-mail: bngl.books@alliedpublishers.com

Website: www.alliedpublishers.com

ISBN: 978-93-89934-72-4

Published by Sunil Sachdev and printed by Ravi Sachdev at Allied Publishers Pvt. Ltd.,
D-5, Sector-2, Noida–201 301

Marketing in the Digital Age: Navigating Disruptions and Embracing Innovations

Organising Committee

(MICA ICMC 2025)

CONFERENCE CHAIRS

Varsha Jain, ***Ph.D.***
AGK Chair Professor of Marketing
MICA, Ahmedabad

Amit Karamchandani
Assistant Professor
MICA, Ahmedabad

COMMITTEE MEMBERS

Manisha Pathak-Shelat, ***Ph.D.***
Professor, MICA, Ahmedabad

Rajneesh Krishna, ***Ph.D.***
Professor, MICA, Ahmedabad

Suresh Malodia, ***Ph.D.***
Associate Professor, MICA, Ahmedabad

Santosh Patra, ***Ph.D.***
Associate Professor, MICA, Ahmedabad

CONFERENCE SECRETARY

Rahul Gadekar
Research Executive, MICA, Ahmedabad

Editorial Committee

(MICA ICMC 2025)

EDITORS

Varsha Jain, *Ph.D.*
AGK Chair Professor of Marketing
MICA, Ahmedabad

Amit Karamchandani, *Ph.D.*
Assistant Professor
MICA, Ahmedabad

EDITORIAL TEAM

Rahul Gadekar
Research Executive
MICA, Ahmedabad

Shruti Kulkarni
Research Assistant
MICA, Ahmedabad

Pooja Singhal
Research Assistant
MICA, Ahmedabad

About the Editors

Dr. Varsha Jain

Prof. Varsha Jain is the AGK chair professor of marketing and co-chairperson of research and dissertation at the MICA, India. She is the deputy editor of the Journal of Consumer Behaviour (JCB, "A" Journal) and an associate editor (AE) at three "A" journals: Psychology and Marketing, the Journal of Consumer Marketing, and the Australasian Marketing Journal. She received the best AE award from JCB in 2022, was an editorial board member at the International Journal of Information Management (A* Journal) and Journal of Business Research (A journal, social media track), and co-track chairperson at the Advertising Academy of Marketing Science, USA, the annual conference, 2023 and co-chairperson, special session, American Marketing Association Winter Conference, 2024. She has authored over 150+ publications (primarily qualitative research in the digital age), including multiple papers in A* and A journals, including the European Journal of Marketing, the International Journal of Information Management, the Journal of Advertising Research, the Journal of Consumer Behavior, the Journal of Consumer Marketing, and the Journal of Business Research.

She has received over 27 international and national awards and gold medals in scholarship. The most recent is the 2024 Best Paper award for a special session held at Winter AMA 2024 at AMA Annual Conference, USA, 2024; the Best Methodology Paper Award at Newcastle University along with Lanchester University Management School and Brunel University, UK (2023) at Marketing, Strategy, and Policy (MSP) Conference, UK and Best Paper (Runner-up) award for a special session held at Winter AMA 2023 at AMA Annual Conference, USA.

In her global research career, she is a visiting guest at Emory Business School, Atlanta, Michigan State University, University of Washington, USA, a visiting scholar at Greenwich University, London, and The Medill School, Northwestern University, USA. Her interests are advertising, branding, consumer behaviour, and digital marketing, primarily immersive technologies, including Artificial Intelligence (Al), Augmented Reality, Virtual Reality, and Metaverse. She is also co-editor for seven special issues related to Al, social media influencers, and Metaverse for JCB in the

"A" journals in 2024 and 2025. She has co-authored and co-edited books, primarily with Prof. Jag Sheth, Consumer Behaviour, Al and Services, Customer Services in Digital Context, and Purpose-driven Branding with Prof. David Aaker. With these global legends, she is working on seven more books related to Al and marketing, global digital consumer behaviour, and customer relationship marketing in the digital context, Aaker on branding, sub-categories of brands, and other international scholars on qualitative research in the digital world and brand India.

Dr. Amit Karamchandani

Amit Karamchandani is an Assistant Professor of Operations Management and Quantitative Techniques in the Business Management area at MICA Ahmedabad. He has a Ph.D. from the Indian Institute of Management, Lucknow (India), and is a graduate (B.Tech) in Mechanical Engineering from IIT (BHU) Varanasi. He has more than 15 years of experience in teaching, research, and industry.

Amit Karamchandani is an Assistant Professor of Operations Management and Quantitative Techniques in the Business Management area at MICA Ahmedabad. He has a Ph.D. from the Indian Institute of Management, Lucknow (India), and is a graduate (B.Tech) in Mechanical Engineering from IIT (BHU) Varanasi. His research interests include Supply chain management, Blockchain, Digital Transformation, Structural equation modeling (SEM), Experimental design, Game Theory and Decision support systems. He has more than 15 years of experience in teaching, research, and industry. He has worked for business schools such as the International Management Institute, New Delhi, and the Great Lakes Institute of Management, Gurgaon. He has seven years of industry experience with Bharat Heavy Electricals Limited (BHEL). He worked on several projects at BHEL aimed at business process digitization. He has published in several ABDC A* and A category international peer-reviewed journals such as Transportation Research Part E: Logistics and Transportation Review (TR-E), International Journal of Information Management (IJIM), International Journal of Production Research (IJPR), Computers and Industrial Engineering (CAIE), and International Journal of Technology, Intelligence, and Planning (IJTIP). His work has been presented at several reputed conferences, such as POMS, ICESCO, ISDSI, and SOM.

Message from the Conference Chairs

(MICA ICMC 2025)

Dear Esteemed Colleagues and Participants,

With great pleasure and honour, we welcome you to the International Communication Management Conference, MICA ICMC 2025. This year's conference promises to be an international, exciting, and enriching experience, bringing together leading global editors, scholars, experts, researchers, and practitioners worldwide to share their insights and advancements in marketing, primarily in the AI world.

Our theme for this year, "Marketing in the Digital Age, Navigating Disruptions and Embracing Innovations," reflects our discipline's dynamic and evolving nature. We have curated a diverse program with guidance from the 14 global advisory members comprising eminent academic personalities from the marketing domain across the globe. The conference program includes keynote speeches, panel discussions, workshops, book launches, and paper presentations designed to develop collaboration, innovation, and knowledge exchange.

We received a total of 352 submissions authored by academicians from India and across the world. The authors represented a total of 19 countries. There were eleven tracks of the conference covering different aspects of marketing in the digital age. A total of 33 expert marketing researchers across the world chaired these tracks and looked after the review process of submissions of their respective tracks. A total of 125 reviewers from MICA, India, and across the world supported the review process.

Overall, the MICA ICMC 2025 features the following events. The YSRC (Young Scholars' Research Colloquium) will happen on Day One and will comprise panel discussions, book launches and workshops. Editors and associate editors of the highly ranked ABDC and Scopus-listed journals will address the emerging scholars during the event. These editors will guide participants in conceptualising research ideas, maintaining methodological rigour in research, and crafting manuscripts for top-tier publications. This will be one of the rare opportunities for emerging scholars to have guidance, network, and collaborate. Day Two will have the formal inauguration of the conference, including keynote addresses by Prof. Russell Belk (Schulich School of Business, Canada) and Mr. Dilip Krishnan (VATIC AI, Singapore), who will address the gathering and share their distinguished expertise in the fields of Marketing and AI. The day will also include various panel discussions and academic paper presentations.

Day Three will continue with academic paper presentations, panel discussions, and a book publication event. A total of 14 well-known marketing academicians across the world and seven industry panellists will participate in the panel discussions.

We encourage all participants to take full advantage of the opportunities presented at this conference. Engage in meaningful discussions, network with peers, and explore new ideas that will drive our field forward.

We want to thank our distinguished speakers, dedicated organising committee, reviewers, authors, and generous sponsors for their invaluable contributions. Their efforts have been instrumental in making this conference a reality.

Sincerely,

MICA ICMC 2025 Conference Chairs,

Dr. Varsha Jain
Dr. Amit Karamchandani

Global Advisory Board Members

(MICA ICMC 2025)

Prof. Jacqueline Eastman
Florida Gulf Coast University, USA

Prof. Ian Phau
Curtin University, Australia

Prof. Liem Viet Ngo
University of New South Wales, Australia

Prof. Renana Peres
Hebrew University, Israel

Prof. Giampaolo Viglia
University of Portsmouth, UK

Prof. Neel Das
Appalachian State University, USA

Prof. Mujde Yuksel
Suffolk University, USA

Dr. Githa Heggde
MICA, India

Prof. Russell Belk
Schulich School of Business,
York University, Canada

Prof. David Aaker
Haas School of Business, University of
California, Berkeley, USA

Prof. Altaf Merchant
Milgard School of Business, University of
Washington, Tacoma, USA

Prof. Rajan Varadarajan
Texas A&M University,
USA

Prof. Rajat Panwar
Oregon State University,
USA

Prof. Jochen Wirtz
National University of Singapore,
Singapore

Prof. Steven D'Alessandro
Edith Cowan University, Australia

Tracks and Track Chairs

(MICA ICMC 2025)

Track 1. **Consumer Behavior in the Digital Context**

- Anupama Ambika, IMT Dubai
- Sanjeev Tripathi, Indian Institute of Management, Indore, India
- Valentina Pitardi, University of Surrey, UK

Track 2. **Digital Marketing Strategies**

- Sigma Soni, Symbiosis University, Pune, India
- Anuj Kapoor Indian Institute of Technology, Jodhpur, India
- Park Thaichon, University of Southern Queensland, Australia

Track 3. **Marketing Analytics**

- Rahul Kumar, Indian Institute of Management, Calcutta, India
- Abhishek Behl, Keele University, UK
- Patrick Van Esch, Coastal Carolina University, USA

Track 4. **Marketing Communication and Advertising**

- Karman Khanna, Goa Institute of Management, Goa, India
- Akshaya Vijayalakshmi, Indian Institute of Management, Ahmedabad, India
- George Spais, Hellenic Open University, Greece

Track 5. **AI with newer technology**

- Khayti Jagani, Flame University
- Raffaele Filieri, Audencia Business School, Italy
- Yogesh Diwedi, Swansea University, UK

Track 6. **Branding in the digital age**

- Cynthia Assaf, ESSCA Business School, France
- Ankur Kapoor, Indian Institute of Management, Udaipur, India
- Omkumar Krishnan, Indian Institute of Management, Kozhikode, India

Track 7. **B2B Marketing and Supply Chain Management in the New Age of Digitization**

- Rahul Sindhwani, Indian Institute of Management, Sambalpur, India
- Amol Dhaigude, SP Jain Institute of Management, India
- Surajit Bag, Excelia Business School, France

Track 8. **Marketing with Augmented Reality, Mixed Reality, Augmented Reality, Extended Reality and Metaverse**

- Margot Racat, IDRAC Business School, France
- Dharun Kasalingam, Indian Institute of Management, Kozhikode, India
- Lim Weng Marc, Sunway University, Malaysia

Track 9. **Marketing and Sustainability**

- Sianne Gordon-Wilson, Queen Mary University of London, UK
- Anand Jaiswal, Indian Institute of Management, Ahmedabad, India
- Pratik Modi, IRMA, Anand, India

Track 10. **Omni Channels and Retailing**

- Shehzala, Faculty, BITS School of Management, Mumbai
- Abhishek Mishra, Indian Institute of Management, Indore, India
- Philipp Brüggemann, University of Hagen, Germany

Track 11. **Services Marketing**

- Emmanuel Mogaji, Keele University, UK
- Sanjit Roy, Edith Cowan University, Australia
- Werner Kunz, University of Massachusetts, USA

Acknowledgement

The MICA ICMC 2025 Organizing Committee takes this opportunity to thank all the Governing Council Members, the Director and CEO of MICA, Ms. Jaya Deshmukh, and the Dean of MICA, Dr. Githa Heggde, for their encouragement and support for MICA ICMC 2025.

Our deepest gratitude goes to the Global Advisory Members for their invaluable insights and continuous support in ensuring the global relevance and excellence of this conference. We sincerely thank the Track Chairs for their time and efforts in conducting the review process and curating the conference sessions. We sincerely acknowledge and thank the reviewers for their rigorous evaluation of submissions, which ensured the high quality of the conference content.

We deeply value our academic and publication partners for their association with the conference and valuable collaboration. We are also grateful to our sponsors for their generous support for the conference.

We sincerely acknowledge the cooperation and contributions of all faculty and staff members of MICA, whose efforts were integral to the success of this event.

Thanks, are also due to Ms. Shruti Kulkarni and Ms. Pooja Singhal for their assistance in the preparation of this Book of Abstracts.

Finally, we appreciate the active involvement of the research team and FPM students of MICA, whose dedication played a significant role in the seamless organization of MICA ICMC 2025.

Thank you to all who contributed to the success of this conference.

Sincerely,

Organizing Committee
MICA ICMC 2025

Contents

TRACK 2

Digital Marketing Strategies

TRACK 3

Marketing Analytics

TRACK 4

Marketing Communication and Advertising

TRACK 5

Artificial Intelligence with Newer Technology

TRACK 6

Branding in the Digital Age

TRACK 7

B2B Marketing and Supply Chain Management in the New Age of Digitization

TRACK 8

Marketing with Augmented Reality, Mixed Reality, Augmented Reality, Extended Reality and Metaverse

TRACK 10

Omni Channels and Retailing

TRACK 11

Services Marketing

TRACK 1

Consumer Behavior in the Digital Context

Intelligent System Framework for Enhancing Digital Payment Adoption among the Youth

Meisya Nurahmasari[1], Christian Haposan Pangaribuan[2] and Tri Wismiarsi[3]

Given the contemporary trend delineating a decline in the utilization of digital payment, this study explores the factors influencing the intention and use of younger generations in the Jakarta area towards digital payment methods. The data collection method uses a quantitative approach and continues with the data analysis method using the Smart-PLS application. Drawing from the empirical evidence from 200 respondents pertaining to Generation Z and Millennials, the study investigates the impact of three key constructs—social influence, facilitating conditions, and promotional activities—on behavioral intention and use behavior towards digital payment. All hypothesized paths were positively significant, suggesting a complex interplay of factors influencing behavioral intention. Notably, facilitating conditions emerge as the most influential factor in driving the intention to use digital payment methods among the youth. Moreover, behavioral intention is identified as a crucial determinant in fostering the adoption of digital payment methods. This study offers valuable insights for policymakers, businesses and marketers seeking to revitalize digital payment adoption and underscores the importance of addressing factors such as technological infrastructure, security concerns, and financial literacy to encourage a cashless society in Jakarta. Theoretically, the suggested results will contribute to the growing body of knowledge aimed at understanding digital payment consumers' behavior through the consistent clustering of behavioral prior experience.

Keywords: *Digital Payment, Use of Technology, Social Influence, Facilitating Conditions, Promotional Activities.*

---

[1] Sampoerna University, Jakarta, Indonesia.
E-mail: meisya.nurahmasari@my.sampoernauniversity.ac.id

[2] Christian Haposan Pangaribuan, Universitas Bunda Mulia, Jakarta, Indonesia.
E-mail: cpangaribuan@bundamulia.ac.id

[3] Sampoerna University, Jakarta, Indonesia. E-mail: tri.wismiarsi@sampoernauniversity.ac.id

Navigating Customer Engagement: Gamification Strategies and Customer Dynamics in FinTech

Ritu Sharma[1] and Reenu Yadav[2]

Customers are more inclined to interact with a firm that provides exciting and pleasurable experiences, resulting in higher customer engagement and a better connection to the brand. Practitioners and researchers seek efficient ways to promote and maintain customer involvement. Gamification extends beyond consumer involvement by including feedback systems, interactivity, and a collaborative component in knowledge exchange for customers and marketers. This paper examines existing literature to establish a strategy for using gamification in the fintech business and contribute to developing theory on this subject. The paper provides an organised, retrospective view of historical theories, factors, and antecedents utilising the TCCM framework and PRISMA. This paper proposes a conceptual model based on the SOR framework for understanding gamification activity and customer experience behaviour. The model also captures outcomes such as rewards, relationships, loyalty, and repeat interactions.

Keywords: *Gamification, Customer Engagement, Customer Experience, Fintech.*

[1] Manav Rachna International Institute for Research and Studies, Faridabad, India. E-mail: scholar.ritusharma@gmail.com

[2] Amity University Haryana, Gurgaon, India. E-mail: 11renurao@gmail.com

[Submission ID 1647 • Track 1]

The Role of De-influencers in Shaping Meaningful Consumer Purchase Decisions

Nishtha Khurana[1] and Varsha Jain[2]

Social media influencers have significantly impacted the behavior of consumers in terms of purchases due to the sheer explosion in the number of social media influencers. Nonetheless, oversaturation of endorsement is contributing to growing scepticism and distrust among consumers. This study explores this emergent phenomenon of de-influencers-those interested in authenticity and purposeful consumption rather than the regular methods of promotion. Whether de-influencers might be able to influence the trust of consumers and also lead to more reflective purchase decisions by means of transparent, value-adding information.

This research uses the mixed-methods approach, applying qualitative insights from interviews conducted with senior practitioners in the area of influencer marketing, and a survey framework in engaging Generation Z consumers who follow de-influencers. The study would make use of thematic analysis in identifying key factors affecting consumer trust and purchase behavior. Source Credibility Theory, Social Influence Theory, Meaning Making Theory, and Para-social Theory are going to be foundational frameworks in interpreting how de-influencers could shape consumer perceptions and decision-making.

The study contributes to the development of extant literature in influencer marketing by bringing theoretical insights into the relatively recent phenomenon of de-influencing. It introduces a framework by which de-influencers could potentially push for authentic engagement and reflective consumption within social commerce. For the brands, the insights will have practical applications to foster trust and align with consumers who prefer ethical and sustainable practice.

Keywords: *De-influencers, Consumer Trust, Social Commerce, Meaningful Consumption, Influencer Marketing.*

[1]MICA, Ahmedabad, India. E-mail: nishthakhurana.23@micamail.in

[2]MICA, Ahmedabad, India. E-mail: varsha.jain@micamail.in

The Impact of Fashion Shopping on Consumer Behavior: Stressor or Stress Reliever?

Shivangi Bhadouria[1] and Chetna Mongna[2]

Shopping has become the most common activity in this digital age mostly in fashion; people use digital and traditional platforms for apparel shopping every day. But did it have a negative impact too? Impacting mental health, concerns of raising the question whether shopping is a stress giver or stress reliever. Many customers engage in shopping trends as a stress reliever and find it a source of happiness, calling it 'Retail therapy'. Buying and acquiring desired items provides a temporary escape from daily pressure. However, digital overload or overconsumption of online shopping has also become a discomfort for some individuals and morphed into a source of anxiety. This research aims to understand how stress affects shopping habits, focusing on young adults; factors such as age, gender, and income are also taken into consideration to know how people shop when they are stressed. This study will explore the dual nature of apparel shopping in the post-pandemic landscape, focusing on its emotional implications, especially among specific demographic groups. In the digital era, shopping has become easier, but it might also affect the mental well-being of consumers in a complex way. This study will focus on why these changes happen and look at the negative effects of shopping on mental health, such as the stress caused by having too many choices and anxiety related to shopping. Moreover, revenge shopping has also materialized after covid-19, where consumers pamper themselves with luxury and comfort. This study tries to fill the gap in research by examining how stress impacts online and offline apparel shopping behaviour.

This research at large aims to provide an understanding of the role and impact of stress on apparel shopping, especially in today's changing retail environment. The research objective is to develop a sustainable approach to consumerism that helps the overall well-being in an increasingly interconnected world.

To address the research objective, the study uses the mixed-method approach. The researcher takes a mixed-research design that is sequential explanatory design where the collection and analysis of qualitative data are done before the quantitative data are collected and analyzed. This approach allows for the development of insights from

[1] FLAME University, Pune, India. E-mail: shivangi.bhadouria@flame.edu.in

[2] FLAME University, Pune, India. E-mail: chetna.monga@flame.edu.in

qualitative data about the fashion shopping journey of the Indian consumer, offline and online, and its impact on their well-being. Insights from the qualitative study will contribute to the creation of hypotheses and the design of the quantitative survey for generalizations of findings.

The goal is to learn more about why they shop and how their emotions affect their decisions. Overall, attaining a balance between enjoying the perks of shopping and managing its stress-inducing aspects is crucial for maintaining mental well-being in the digital period Ultimately, this research aims to provide a clearer picture of how stress and shopping are connected, especially in today's changing retail environment. The motive is to develop a sustainable approach to digital consumerism that helps the overall well-being of an increasingly interconnected world.

Keywords: *Online Shopping, Offline Consumption, Online Shopping and Mental Health, Consumer Behavior after COVID-19, Stress and Health.*

Is it Fake or Real? Young Consumer's Brand Trust Through Deepfake Video Content

Darshi Hingrajia[1] and Khyati Jagani[2]

Deepfake videos are lifelike videos that show celebrities, public figures, and prominent politicians making announcements or statements or promoting a product or service. These lifelike videos seem authentic, but they are created using artificial intelligence that manipulates facial expressions and lip sync to match voice-over audio. The existence of deepfake videos can be traced to a video on Reddit in 2017. In advertising, brands like Coca-Cola have begun to use artificial intelligence to recreate their classic advertisements. On the other spectrum, fake brands, pirate websites, and fraudulent companies create deepfake videos that showcase a prominent business leader/politician vouching for a product or service. Such videos can impact the viewers, especially the younger generation, who would not know that the video is fake and would trust the information provided by the public figure. It poses a critical challenge and threat to young consumers' brand perception. The study aims to evaluate the role played by deepfake videos portrayed as advertisements on the brand perception of young consumers.

Keywords: *Deepfake, Misinformation, Brand Trust, Brand Credibility, Consumer Perception.*

[1]FLAME University, Pune, India. E-mail: darshi.hingrajia@flame.edu.in

[2]FLAME University, Pune, India. E-mail: khyati.jagani@flame.edu.in

[Submission ID 3392 • Track 1]

Impact of FinFluencers on Modern Investment Decisions

Radhesh Shah[1], Rashi Shah[2], Shivika Agarwal[3] and Yuvraj Khetan[4]

The rise of financial influencers, or "FinFluencers," on social media platforms like Instagram, YouTube, Facebook and LinkedIn has significantly impacted modern investment decisions in India. This research paper explores the influence of FinFluencers on investment behaviours by analysing data from over 100 investors. Key metrics includes information dissemination on social media, engagement levels (likes, views, comments) and the difference in monetary impact on FinFluencer & Non-FinFluencer audiences. The study examines how FinFluencers affect investors' risk appetites both positively and negatively and the need for regulatory oversight. Our findings through statistical tools like Regression & T-test, suggest that FinFluencers play a crucial role in shaping investment strategies nowadays. But there is a need for these influencers to adhere to SEBI-registered marketing methods to ensure ethical and informed investment advice.

Keywords: *FinFluencer, Social Media Marketing, Investment Decisions, Investor Behaviour, Risk Appetite, SEBI Regulations, Ethical Investment Advice.*

[1] Institute of Management, Nirma University, Ahmedabad, India.
E-mail: 227356@nirmauni.ac.in

[2] Institute of Management, Nirma University, Ahmedabad, India.
E-mail: 227359@nirmauni.ac.in

[3] Institute of Management, Nirma University, Ahmedabad, India.
E-mail: 227370@nirmauni.ac.in

[4] Institute of Management, Nirma University, Ahmedabad, India.
E-mail: 227380@nirmauni.ac.in

The Role of Technology in Shaping Consumer Satisfaction in Quick Commerce: Insights from Digital Consumer Behavior

Punnesh Nagori[1] and Prathamesh Khadge[2]

The retail landscape has been significantly disrupted by the rise of quick commerce (q-commerce), which provides near-instant deliveries through technology-driven platforms. Technological factors such as app interface, usability, real-time tracking, and personalized product recommendations heavily influence consumer satisfaction in this digital age. This study seeks to explore the impact of these innovations on consumer behavior and satisfaction within the fast-paced quick-commerce sector. It aims to investigate how consumers interact with technology on quick commerce platforms and how it shapes their overall satisfaction levels. The study focuses on key digital features like app navigation, real-time tracking, personalized recommendations, and customer support to identify which technological innovations most significantly influence consumer behavior. It also examines how these features are transforming shopping patterns and consumer expectations, offering valuable insights for q-commerce platforms to navigate and adapt to the rapidly evolving market landscape. To gather insights, a quantitative survey was conducted with around 200 participants who regularly use q-commerce services such as Zepto, Blinkit, and Instamart. The survey looked into how frequently consumers used these platforms, their satisfaction with the technological features, and their overall experience. The responses were measured using a Likert scale (1–5) to assess satisfaction levels, and the data was analyzed to determine correlations between the use of specific features and overall consumer satisfaction. Descriptive statistics and regression analysis were applied to identify the most influential factors driving satisfaction. The findings of the study indicate that the ease of app navigation and the accuracy of real-time order tracking are the most critical factors driving consumer satisfaction, with over 75% of respondents rating them as highly important (4–5 on the scale). While 60% of respondents appreciated personalized product recommendations, they had less impact

[1] Prin. L.N. Welingkar Institute of Management, Mumbai, India.
E-mail: 1rba2024-punnesh.nagori@welingkar.org

[2] Prin. L.N. Welingkar Institute of Management, Mumbai, India.
E-mail: 1rba2024-prathamesh.khadge@welingkar.org

on purchasing behavior, with only 30% of respondents regularly purchasing suggested products. Furthermore, strong customer support and timely issue resolution emerged as key contributors to overall satisfaction, highlighting the continued importance of human interaction, even within technology-driven services. This research underscores the essential role of technology in shaping satisfaction within the quick commerce sector in the context of digital consumer behavior. It emphasizes the need for q-commerce platforms to prioritize seamless app navigation, precise real-time tracking, and responsive customer support to meet growing consumer demands. The study also points to the need for refining personalized product suggestions to increase their relevance and impact on purchase decisions. By embracing technological innovations and addressing these critical factors, q-commerce platforms can better navigate the disruptions of the digital age, ultimately driving stronger consumer loyalty and long-term engagement. This research provides actionable insights for q-commerce businesses operating in the digital context, offering a roadmap to enhance consumer satisfaction through technology. Platforms that integrate user-friendly design, real-time services, and personalized experiences are well-positioned to thrive in the competitive landscape of the digital age as consumer expectations continue to evolve.

Keywords: *Quick Commerce, Consumer Behavior, Digital Platform, Technological Innovation, Customer Satisfaction.*

Unveiling the Role of Masstige, Experience and Values on eWOM Towards Masstige Service Brands in the Digital Age: An Extended Abstract

Loveleen Kaur[1] and Pavleen Soni[2]

Recognizing the significance of eWOM in the digital age and growing masstige market, this study explores how masstige, experience, and perceived consumption values shape eWOM intentions. Grounded in masstige theory and cue utilization theory, our research employs a two-level data collection approach. Initially, it identifies prominent masstige brands, followed by purposive sampling of respondents who have visited one of the selected coffee chain outlets. Through structural equation modeling, we evaluate our conceptual model, revealing key relationships between the identified variables. The findings provide valuable theoretical insights and practical implications for masstige marketers, highlighting strategies to enhance customer engagement and retention. Additionally, it examines the moderating effects of demographics, offering a nuanced understanding of how different consumer segments engage with eWOM. This research contributes to the broader discourse on digital marketing and masstige marketing in the hospitality industry, emphasizing the critical role of eWOM in shaping consumer perceptions and driving business success in a competitive landscape.

Keywords: *Masstige, Prestige Brands, Ewom, Consumption Values, Experience.*

[1]Guru Nanank Dev University, Amritsar, India.
E-mail: loveleenubs.rsh@gndu.ac.in

[2]Guru Nanak Dev University, Amritsar, India. E-mail: pavleen.soni@gmail.com

[Submission ID 4998 • Track 1]

Exploring Consumer Behaviour & Key Influences on Adoption in the Rapidly Growing Quick Commerce Industry

Akshay Jain[1], Saransh Vashishta[2] and Tarun Pratap Singh[3]

Introduction: As the digital economy continues to evolve, the Quick Commerce sector has emerged as a key player in meeting the growing demand for convenience and speed in everyday shopping. Platforms like Blink it, Zepto, and Swiggy Instamart promise ultra-fast delivery, often within minutes, reshaping consumer expectations for immediacy. This shift is particularly significant as consumers increasingly seek faster, more efficient ways to obtain daily necessities, driven by factors such as busy lifestyles, urbanisation, and technological advancements. The rapid rise of Quick Commerce, offering ultra-fast delivery of everyday goods, is reshaping consumer shopping behaviour. This research aims to explore consumer preferences and behaviour in this growing sector, focusing on factors such as platform preference, product types, frequency of use, and satisfaction with service attributes like delivery speed, pricing, and convenience.

Purpose: The purpose of this research is to understand consumer preferences and behaviour in the growing Quick Commerce sector, which offers ultra-fast delivery of everyday goods. The study aims to explore various factors that influence consumer decisions, such as platform preference, product types, frequency of use, and satisfaction with service attributes like delivery speed, pricing, and convenience. The insights gathered from this research will provide a comprehensive understanding of the key drivers behind consumer adoption of Quick Commerce, including the impact of surge charges on purchasing decisions. Additionally, the study will evaluate consumer satisfaction levels in comparison to traditional e-commerce services. The findings will contribute to academic discussions on consumer behaviour in emerging digital markets and offer valuable implications for businesses seeking to enhance their Quick Commerce offerings, thus shaping the future of the industry.

[1]Welingkar Institute of Management Development and Research Mumbai, India.
E-mail: akshayjain0109@gmail.com

[2]Welingkar Institute of Management Development and Research Mumbai, India.
E-mail: saransh.sharma27@gmail.com

[3]Welingkar Institute of Management Development and Research Mumbai, India.
E-mail: tarunpratap24@gmail.com

Method: Descriptive research and quantitative methodologies were utilized to assess consumer opinions regarding behaviour and preferences in the Quick Commerce sector. A survey using a structured questionnaire was conducted to collect insights into consumer choices, purchasing habits, and satisfaction with Quick Commerce services. Voluntary participants aged 18 to 35 and above were included in the study, with a sample size of 200 respondents. Statistical tools such as chi-square and Spearman correlation were applied to analyse the relationships between different independent and dependent variables, offering a deeper understanding of the factors influencing consumer behaviour in this fast-paced market.

Findings: Buying Behaviour, Customer Preference, Influencing Factors, Further Scope for High-Value Categories, Surge Charge and Price Sensitivity, Delivery Charges and Average Order Value

Conclusion: This research offers valuable insights into consumer behaviour in the rapidly expanding Quick Commerce sector. Key findings indicate that delivery speed, pricing strategies (including surge charges), and product availability significantly influence consumer decisions and satisfaction. Consumers increasingly prefer platforms that prioritize convenience and speed, essential for Quick Commerce success. The study also highlights the impact of surge pricing, noting that some consumers are sensitive to price fluctuations during peak times.

Keywords: *Consumer Behaviour, Customer Preference, Price Sensitivity, Surge Charge Effect, Average Order Value.*

Examining Luxury Democratization and Impression Management Motivations on Consumers' Behavioral Intentions

Paurav Shukla[1] and Veronica Rosendo-Rios[2]

Middle-class consumers account for nearly half of the luxury goods market globally, with this segment expected to be expanding to 450 million by 2025 (D'Arpizio *et al.*, 2020). To satiate the needs of this segment who demands access and equality, many luxury goods firms have changed their strategies and developed product offerings that have resulted in once inaccessible and highly exclusive goods become available to the masses in a process of luxury democratization, understood as consumers' attempt to create equality of access to purchase or wear luxury goods that results in greater perceived availability, and reduced distinctiveness, exclusivity and self-differentiation. Yet, the study of traditional luxury consumers' perception of this new luxury goods landscape has been largely ignored. Grounded on the theory of network effects and the theory of impression management, this study provides empirical evidence in understanding the effects of luxury democratization on traditional luxury consumer behavioral intentions and how they are channeled through indulgence and mitigated by impression management motives. This research provides actionable insights for luxury companies to refine their positioning strategies, enabling them to navigate the challenges posed by luxury democratization.

Keywords: *Luxury, Branding, Democratization, Impression Management.*

[1] University of Southampton, Southampton, United Kingdom. E-mail: p.v.shukla@soton.ac.uk

[2] Universidad Pontificia Comillas, Madrid, Spain. E-mail: vrosendo@comillas.edu

Exploring Consumer Purchase Intent for Rental Goods through Social Media Influence

Pooja Singhal[1], Vineet Vinny[2] and Mini Mathur[3]

The rental goods market has expanded rapidly, driven by evolving consumer preferences, sustainability concerns, and the growing influence of social media. This study explores consumer purchase intent for rental goods, focusing on platforms like Instagram and Facebook. It aims to analyze the economic, social, and environmental value consumers associate with rentals, examine how businesses engage users through shoppable posts and influencer collaborations, and assess how different types of social media influencers impact rental decisions. A review of the literature reveals that sectors such as fashion, electronics, and furniture dominate the online rental market, with fashion rentals leading due to their visual appeal on social platforms (Tussyadiah, 2016). Renting is becoming a preferred option as it offers lower upfront costs, access to high-quality products without long-term ownership, and protection from depreciation (Belk, 2014). Renting also aligns with minimalist lifestyles, reduces storage needs, and supports sustainability by contributing to the circular economy (Heinrichs, 2013). This research draws on the Theory of Planned Behavior (TPB) and Theory of Reasoned Action (TRA). TPB suggests that consumer intent is influenced by attitudes, social norms, and perceived behavioral control (Ajzen, 1991). TRA emphasizes the role of subjective norms and individual attitudes in shaping behavior. These frameworks are essential to understanding how consumers engage with rental services, especially through social media, where influencers and peer opinions play a crucial role in decision-making. A mixed-methods approach will be adopted, combining quantitative surveys and qualitative interviews. Quantitative data will be collected via surveys to assess consumer attitudes, subjective norms, perceived control, and tendencies toward instant gratification. These surveys will also explore how often users rent products after engaging with rental-related content and the impact of peer reviews or influencer endorsements. Stratified sampling will ensure diverse representation across demographic groups, allowing for in-depth analysis of rental behavior. Qualitative data will be gathered through social media interactions of the accounts of rental based services. The content analysis will be done using Posts,

[1]MICA, Ahmedabad, India. E-mail: pooja.singhal@micamail.in

[2]MICA, Ahmedabad, India. E-mail: vineet.vinny@micamail.in

[3]MICA, Ahmedabad, India. E-mail: mini.mathur@micamail.in

comments, and reviews on platforms and will be analyzed to uncover themes like instant gratification, sustainability, and cost-saving etc. In-depth interviews will explore consumers' motivations for renting, focusing on social norms and personal experiences. Additionally, engagement metrics such as likes, shares, and clicks on rental-related posts will provide insights into behavioral patterns. This research will offer valuable insights for both academics and practitioners. It will enhance understanding of the values driving rental choices and highlight effective engagement strategies for businesses. These findings can guide companies in leveraging influencer marketing and foster sustainable consumption practices in an evolving rental market.

Keywords: *Rental Goods, Social Media, Consumer Behaviour, Consumer Purchase Intent, Fashion Rentals.*

Impact of Psychographic Variables on Counterfeit Consumption in the Presence of Social Media

Ritu Raj[1]

Social media has become popular in both business and research as many studies have explored the impact of this medium on the purchase behavior of consumers but surprisingly not in the domain of counterfeiting. Social media has become a significant part of today's lifestyle and it has created new channels for brand manufacturers and consumers to communicate. The present study tries to assess the impact of psychographic variables in the presence of social media determinants on counterfeit purchase intention. The study explored different factors of psychographic variables. Further, the study checks for the mediation effect of social media platform in between psychographic variables and purchase intention. The data for the present study were collected from three metropolitan cities of India namely Delhi, Kolkata, and Mumbai. The PLS-SEM was used on 406 respondents for further analysis and validation. The results revealed that there is a significant impact of price consciousness, value consciousness and novelty seeking on consumers' purchase intention towards counterfeit fashion products. However, an insignificant relationship was found between social status and purchase intention. Further, the study suggested that social media platform mediates the relationship between psychographic determinants and the purchase intention of consumers towards the purchase of counterfeit products in India.

Keywords: *Social Media Platform, Counterfeit Products, Purchase Intentions, PLS-Sem.*

[1]Institute of Management, Nirma University, Ahmedabad, India. E-mail: ritu_rs@mba.nits.ac.in

Virtual Companions or Animated Allies? Exploring Trustworthiness, Psychological Closeness, and Companionship with Nearly Human *vs.* Animated Virtual Influencers

Rehan Husain[1] and Shalini Nath Tripathi[2]

The emergence of virtual influencers heralds a paradigm shift in the realm of digital marketing, wielding an unparalleled ability to mold audience perceptions and instigate profound behavioral metamorphoses. Drawing upon ambivalent theory and avatar marketing theory, this paper examined the interaction effect of form realism and perceived homophily of virtual influencers in shaping consumers' perceived trust, warmth, closeness, and, subsequently, companionship induced by VI. The six studies employing experimental materials generated by artificial intelligence were conducted. Study (1–3) for developed countries while studies (4–6) for developing countries. The findings showed significant differences in the perception of VI in developed and developing countries. In developed countries, warmth and closeness play a critical role in inducing companionships by VIs, while in developing countries, it is primarily done by perceived trustworthiness. The research advances the current understanding of the moderation of perceived homophily that serves as a quick route for establishing companionship. These insights offer novel marketing and practical implications for brand managers who aim to leverage the power of virtual influencers.

Keywords: *Virtual Influencers, Homophily, Psychological Closeness, Warmth, Companionship, form Realism.*

[1]Jaipuria Institute of Management, Lucknow, Lucknow, India.
E-mail: rehan.husain@jaipuria.ac.in

[2]Jaipuria Institute of Management, Lucknow, Lucknow, India.
E-mail: shalini.tripathi@jaipuria.ac.in

Gaining a Deeper Understanding of Patient Experiences: The Role of Technology in Empowerment and Care Pathways

Ameni Ben Jebril[1] and Nora Bezaz[2]

The urgency of social distancing during the health crisis highlighted the importance of technological innovation in the medical field, offering new opportunities for patients to access healthcare services through telemedicine and, more broadly, telehealth (Ellouze & Damak, 2022). Patients are also encountering the development of electronic medical records in their care pathways. Digital technology enables remote monitoring of patients while increasing their autonomy in managing their care by facilitating movement and communication with a hospital system (Sunder & Thirumalai, 2024). The French government aims to support investment in technological innovations, a major issue in the healthcare field affecting all stakeholders, including the hospital environment. This research in progress focuses on the behavior and care pathways of the "patient-client" as a consumer of healthcare services in the era of e-health in France. Technological innovation acts as a significant catalyst, redefining how patients navigate their care pathways in hospitals.

In the literature, Carayon and Woldrid (2020) define the patient pathway as the spatio-temporal distribution of patient interactions with multiple healthcare structures over time. In this sense, the patient interacts with various elements of the healthcare system (physicians, nurses, organizations, technology, etc.) during medical care in a healthcare facility. Technology and healthcare are closely intertwined (Pieterse *et al.*, 2018). Healthcare influences how technology is designed, and technology can change how healthcare is organized. Today, patients use technology to communicate with their doctors and manage their care pathways, particularly in cases of chronic illness.

This exploratory study aims to understand how technological innovation impacts the patient pathway in the hospital and medico-social environment. The study is based on semi-structured interviews with a diverse profile (professionals and patients) and a content analysis.

Initial results indicate that innovative tools facilitate the adaptation of procedures to the specific needs of each patient, enhancing the quality of care and reducing recovery

[1] University of Lorraine, Epinal, France. E-mail: ameni.ben-jebril@univ-lorraine.fr

[2] University of Lorraine, Epinal, France. E-mail: nora.bezaz@univ-lorraine.fr

times. Findings show that technological innovation provides benefits at various stages of the patient journey. A connected care pathway affords patients empowerment and enhances their experience. Utilizing technology to facilitate access to care has the potential to reduce time expenditure for all stakeholders. Furthermore, applying artificial intelligence and health data analysis allows for customizing treatments to align with individual patients' specific requirements and preferences. The patient experience plays a key role in participative and collaborative design within the context of the patient pathway. This experience is shaped by various interactions across spatial and temporal dimensions (Beleffi *et al.*, 2022).

From a managerial perspective, to reduce resistance to telemedicine, supporting patients through clear information, training, and personalized assistance is important. Communication tools are essential levers when implementing technological innovation in healthcare organizations.

Controlled technological innovation fosters a virtuous circle that benefits patients, residents, and families. The need to invest in technological innovation for the benefit of both residents and patients represents a major challenge that can reduce future pathology costs, improve working conditions in a pressured profession, and attract residents who are close to total loss of autonomy and can benefit from better care.

Keywords: *Technological Innovations, Patient Empowerment, Patient Journey, Care Pathways, Patient Experience, Qualitative Research.*

[Submission ID 9860 • Track 1]

Price Volatility and Consumer Response in the Digital Economy: An Economic Approach

Rejakshi Ghosh[1] and Rasananda Panda[2]

Digitalisation of services allows goods and services to be offered through both online and offline modes. Since the price flexibility possibly allows firms to capitalise on the price fluctuations, consumers can compare costs and find appropriately priced items online. Unlike traditional methods, which would require reprinting of menu cards or price tags; no or minimal menu costs are accrued as changing prices no longer requires the same processes and prices can be digitally altered. Thus the price change process has significantly changed in the digital economy, affecting consumers. Through an extensive literature review, this study aims to primarily observe and attempt to explain how consumers react and behave in response to price volatility arising out of digitalisation of the economy.

Keywords: *Digitalisation, Digital Economy, Menu Costs, Price Volatility, Consumer Response.*

[1]MICA, Ahmedabad, India. E-mail: rejakshi.ghosh@micamail.in

[2]MICA, Ahmedabad, India. E-mail: rasananda.panda@micamail.in

Effect of Luxury Fashion Content on User Engagement on Instagram

Avantika Nabira[1], Ashna Vig[2], Aman Sakhuja[3] and Priyam Jhunjhunwala[4]

This research explores the impact of luxury fashion content on Instagram user engagement, with a focus on how overexposure to it can lead to negative emotions and shifts in consumer attitudes such as envy, resentment, and content fatigue. The global luxury fashion industry, valued at approximately $450 billion, leverages Instagram to market exclusive brands like Gucci, and Chanel. Although these platforms initially create aspirational appeal, continuous exposure risks alienating users and prompting emotional disengagement. Luxury brands must recognize that unchecked content saturation can result in long-term damage to brand perception, as consumer frustration escalates and engagement declines.

The study uses two psychological frameworks: Uses and Gratifications Theory (UGT) and Social Comparison Theory (SCT). UGT suggests that users engage with luxury content to fulfill social validation and self-esteem needs, viewing luxury goods as symbols of accomplishment. However, this research aims to extend this theory by exploring how, due to overexposure to the content, admiration shifts to envy and frustration, especially when viewers lack access to these lifestyles. SCT explains that Instagram's curated content encourages upward social comparisons, where users compare themselves to more affluent individuals, fostering feelings of inadequacy and dissatisfaction.

This research adopts a descriptive methodology with a multi-method approach, combining netnography to observe and analyze consumer interactions in the digital environment, in-depth interviews to gather qualitative insights into emotional reactions, projective techniques to uncover subconscious attitudes toward luxury fashion, and quantitative surveys to measure the prevalence and intensity of these reactions. These methods collectively provide a detailed framework to understand how luxury content impacts passive observers—users who frequently view but cannot access luxury goods. Findings indicate that while luxury brands aim to evoke

[1]MICA, Ahmedabad, India. E-mail: avantikanabira.24@micamail.in

[2]MICA, Ahmedabad, India. E-mail: ashnavig.24@micamail.in

[3]MICA, Ahmedabad, India. E-mail: amansakhuja.24@micamail.in

[4]MICA, Ahmedabad, India. E-mail: priyamjhunjhunwala.24@micamail.in

admiration, unchecked content exposure can lead to resentment, content fatigue, and eventual disengagement, which poses risks to brand loyalty and market position. This study underscores the importance for brands to balance aspirational content with mindful engagement strategies that mitigate negative emotional responses.

The findings of this research hold valuable lessons for luxury marketers and influencers. More mindful and meaningful strategies can be generated by understanding the emotional impact of overposting, for maintaining the right balance in audience engagement without triggering negative reactions. Recognising this delicate balance between aspiration and alienation is essential for maintaining meaningful consumer connections in an era where Instagram influences perceptions of wealth and prestige. In the scope of academia, this research will serve as a foundation for gaining better understanding of digital users and their attitudes towards the different content that they are exposed to on Instagram. By extension, this research also lays a foundation for understanding other industries in the luxury segment in context to consumer attitudes on social media.

The model developed in this study provides a strategic framework demonstrating how luxury fashion content impacts user engagement by linking social motivations to emotional outcomes. It highlights a cycle where brands adapt strategies in response to user emotions, balancing aspiration with sustained engagement.

Keywords: *Luxury, Fashion, Content, Instagram, User Engagement, Disengagement, Desire, User Disposition.*

TRACK 2

Digital Marketing Strategies

[Submission ID 1962 • Track 2]

Unlocking the Travel Secret: Exploring the Power of Influencers in Driving Travelers to Backpacker Hostels

Shikha Gupta[1], Kartika Chaudhary[2], Anuj Pal Kapoor[3] and Amit Singh[4]

Emerging trend of digital influence is reshaping travelers' behaviour (Armutcu *et al.*, 2023). Social media influencers, through their content, are highlighting affordable accommodations and immersive cultural experiences. The content not only inspires travelers, but also promotes sustainable tourism. As a result, backpacker tourism like Zostel and Hosteller have gained popularity, offering affordable stays, social interaction, and cultural exchange among travelers (Ooi and Laing, 2010). Recognizing the importance of sustainable tourism (Tussyadiah & Sigala, 2018), the United Nations Sustainable Development Goals stress the need to support the development of eco-friendly travel practices (Rej *et al.*, 2022). Thus, through innovative digital marketing strategies in tourism industry, firms have continued to promote sustainable tourism practices (Vinzenz *et al.*, 2019). However, as per our understanding, consumer behaviour in the context of backpacker hostels remains underexplored. Furthermore, there is a research call for exploring the role of digital interactions in shaping tourists behaviour (Armutcu *et al.*, 2023). Thus, this study aims to examine the impact of digital marketing strategies with a focus on influencer marketing on travelers' motivations and intentions to use affordable backpacker hostels.

The conceptual framework illustrates how travelers' motivations to use backpacker hostels, combined with the influence of social media influencers, shape attitudes and ultimately influence the usage intention. To build our conceptual model, we integrated self-determination theory (Deci & Ryan, 2012) and source credibility theory (Birnbaum & Stegner, 1979). According to self-determination theory, there exists intrinsic motivation such as personal satisfaction or enjoyment, including desire to meet new people and seek adventure, and extrinsic motivation such as monetary rewards or peer influence directly influencing travelers' attitudes toward

[1]Indian Institute of Technology Jodhpur, Jodhpur, India. E-mail: gupta.93@iitj.ac.in

[2]Indian Institute of Technology Jodhpur, Jodhpur, India. E-mail: chaudhary.13@iitj.ac.in

[3]Indian Institute of Technology Jodhpur, Jodhpur, India. E-mail: anujkapoor@iitj.ac.in

[4]Amrut Modi School of Management, Ahmedabad University, Ahmedabad, India. E-mail: amtkds@gmail.com

these hostels (Kong *et al.*, 2019). According to source credibility theory, certain factors of social media influencers, such as trustworthiness, expertise, and attractiveness, amplify the influence by shaping travelers' perceptions through their credibility (Balaban & Mustăţea, 2019; Chekima *et al.*, 2020). Depending on their perceived credibility, influencers' endorsements can either strengthen or weaken the attitudes of travelers toward backpacker hostels. The model underscores the importance of both motivation and influencer credibility influencing attitudes that lead to usage intention, highlighting the role of digital marketing in promoting sustainable tourism.

To conduct this study, mixed-method research will be employed. Firstly, a qualitative study comprising interviews of backpacker hostel users. Secondly, an online survey to gather quantitative data about traveler motivation in relation to attitudes and intentions to stay at backpacker hostels. This mixed-method approach will enhance the understanding of motivation and credibility of influencers to help decision-makers in the travel sharing economy.

This study highlights significance of digital marketing in promoting sustainable tourism through social media influencers. By showcasing how influencers gain trust and change consumer decisions, marketers have an opportunity to reach potential travelers in a more efficient way. Businesses can collaborate with trusted influencers to create authentic, engaging content that aligns with travelers' desires for autonomy, social interaction, and budget-friendly experiences. Overall, sharing economy model and focusing on engagement through social media platforms helps to create eco-consciousness and reduce carbon footprints.

Keywords: *Backpackers Hostel, Social Media Influencers, Sharing Economy, Sustainable Tourism, Traveling.*

Examining the Influence of Fear Appeals on Information Privacy Concern and Privacy Protection Intentions among Online Consumers: Applying the Extended Parallel Process Model

Avi Karan[1] and G.K. Murthy[2]

Fear appeal is a persuasive tactic used to promote healthier behaviors. Extensively used in public health and advertising campaigns in the past, fear appeals have recently gained the attention of information security and privacy scholars towards encouraging security and privacy-protective behaviors.

With recent advancements in technology and the increased potential of privacy-related risks, several regulations have been enacted to safeguard online users and regulate businesses. On the contrary, despite concerns about the misuse of personal information, consumers often act paradoxically when sharing information online. Thus, studies on the effectiveness of persuasive appeals to promote privacy-protective behavior are timely and relevant. Limited studies have effectively employed fear appeals in studying privacy-protective behaviours. Moreover, fear appeal-based studies including the role of individual differences such as self-esteem (SE) and dispositional mindfulness (DM) are scarce.

The present study employs a twofold study approach. The first study is a 2 × 2 between-subjects experimental design that investigates the effectiveness of fear appeals on information privacy concerns and privacy protection intentions. The second study employs an online survey to examine the influence of perceived threat (PT), perceived efficacy (PE), SE, and DM using structural equation modeling.

This study provides a comprehensive understanding of how fear appeals work in the context of information privacy among individuals with varying SE. Thus, the study has implications for businesses and regulators towards designing effective marketing campaigns to safeguard consumers. This study also contributes theoretically by

[1]Chandragupt Institute of Management, Patna & Amity University Patna, India. E-mail: f0201@cimp.ac.in

[2]Chandragupt Institute of Management Patna, India. E-mail: murthy.gk@cimp.ac.in

extending the existing literature on fear appeals and individual differences in information privacy context.

Keywords: *Fear Appeals, EPPM, Information Privacy Concerns, Privacy Protective Intentions, Mindfulness, Self Esteem, Quantitative, Experiment, Survey.*

Virtual Reality in the In-store Luxury Shopping Experience: Customers Satisfaction

Serena Rovai[1], Ian Phau[2] and Cecilia Pasquinelli[3]

Although the application of digital technologies accelerated the orientation towards the online retailing journey in the pandemic context, the role of the physical store is still central in luxury shopping. The literature highlighted the growing impact of digital technologies and in particular AI as VR on consumer shopping experiences and retailing. Multiple factors are influencing luxury fashion and certainly technology changes are impacting clients' behaviours and satisfaction, in particular satisfaction of one of the increasing relevant customer segments in luxury, the so-defined millennials.

Digitalisation in luxury has been supported by cultural values in this market (Chen and Zhang, 2011; Kim and Zhang, 2013; Rovai, 2016; Bazi *et al.*, 2020), led by the growing segment of "digital native" millennials whose specificity in luxury shopping habits are discussed in the literature (Ko and Meghee, 2012; Ko and Jang, 2012; Zhang and He, 2012; Faschan *et al.*, 2020), and they are reported to be playing a major role in luxury industry growth (Bazi *et al.*, 2020; Kim, 2020). As a results, digital technologies but more specifically AI derived applications as VR have been acquiring attention in consumer studies (Evanschitzky *et al.*, 2020; Klaus & Zaichkowsky, 2020; Kaplan & Haenlein, 2020; Pantano *et al.*, 2022) and specifically on how these technologies affect customer behavior, influence advertising perception (Jayawardena *et al.*, 2023) and luxury value, providing key insights into how AI-driven experiences can both enhance and sometimes reduce customer engagement in high-end services (Pantano, 2024) and reshaping customers' experiences (Paul, Pantano and Zhang, 2024). In this perspective, contribution of the store to a satisfactory luxury experience specifically for those millennials, but not only, has started to be analysed from different perspectives. The store showed to provide a vital contribution to the luxury experience, being an opportunity to design a personalized and unique moment for consumers (Manthiou, Hickman, and Klaus, 2020).

Consequently, in the fast-emerging VR impact on consumers' behaviour and after reviewing the consumer behaviour and VR stream of research in the luxury sector,

[1]Excelia Group - La Rochelle Business School, France. E-mail: rovais@excelia-group.com

[2]Curtin University, Australia. E-mail: ian.phau@cbs.curtin.edu.au

[3] Università degli Studi Napoli Parthenope, Italy. E-mail: Cecilia.pasquinelli@uniparthenope.it

this study aims to explore the VR impact on the in-store luxury shopping experience influencing the customer behaviour and satisfaction, with a specific focus on the relevant segment of millennials. In particular, the study tries to define the resulting consumers' profiles associated to their in-store VR experience satisfaction. In so doing, through a qualitative methodology based on a multiple data collection approach – survey, focus groups and interviews to international it attempts to fill a still existing gap in literature and give useful management practices.

Keywords: *Digital Strategies, VR, Customer Satisfaction.*

Digital Marketing for the Performing Arts: The Italian Opera Houses' Pandemic Heritage and Beyond

Nicola Bellini[1]

Digital marketing opens new opportunities for dialogue, to intercept younger audiences, that is vital to performing arts, such as opera. Based on the social media strategy adopted by the opera houses to cope with the health emergency during the pandemic, we propose to analyze the heritage of that experience. This implies managerial challenges in managing a 'conversational' relationship with the audience and may coincide with new trends toward a 'phygital' transformation of the theatrical experience.

Keywords: *Digital Marketing, Cultural Institutions, Performing Arts, Opera.*

---

[1]Scuola Superiore Sant'Anna Pisa, Italy. E-mail: n.bellini@santannapisa.it

Visualizing Cold: Uncovering the Sensory Visual Cues that Convey Coldness in Images

Nitya Kumari[1], Bibhas Chandra[2] and Anugrah Narayan Shukla[3]

The photography on social media plays an important role in the purchase decision of consumers. An alluring image of any product on social media creates a desire to have that product. There are lots of cues that will enhance the photography of various foods like fast food, cake, as well as healthy foods. When it comes to cold foods or frozen desserts like ice-creams, smoothies, and chilled beverages, there are very less cold visual cues which will enhance the photography. This study aims to address these gaps by exploring how cold visual cues, such as ice crystals and steamy cold fog, affect consumer perception of cold foods using eye-tracking technology. Through eye-tracking, we get to know that participants will exhibit longer fixation on cold visual cues. The questionnaire will provide insights about the perceived experience of the consumers. Cold visual cues might increase the food desirability and willingness to pay (WTP). The current study highlights the increasing importance of food photography on social media and the growing food e-commerce or retail industry. From a theoretical point of view, this research will contribute to the growing body of literature on cold food products, sensory marketing, and multisensory perception, by providing deeper insight on understanding of how coldness is visually perceived and processed by consumers.

Keywords: *Gastronomy, Online Food Marketing, Sensory Marketing, Sensory Cues, Eye-tracking.*

[1]IIT (ISM), Dhanbad, Dhanbad, India. E-mail: 22dr0154@iitism.ac.in

[2] IIT (ISM), Dhanbad, Dhanbad, India. E-mail: bibhaschandra@iitism.ac.in

[3] IIT (ISM), Dhanbad, Dhanbad, India. E-mail: 22dr0019@iitism.ac.in

TRACK 3

Marketing Analytics

[Submission ID 2226 • Track 3]

The Impact of Marketing Analytics on Business Performance: Navigating Consumer Insights and Ethical Considerations

Aman Dwivedi[1], Shagun Rana[2] and Sahil Jain[3]

Introduction: In the rapidly evolving digital landscape, Marketing Analytics has emerged as a pivotal resource for businesses striving to leverage data effectively. This study investigates how organizations can utilize analytics to refine their marketing strategies, foster deeper customer relationships, and enhance overall business performance. As consumer behaviors become increasingly multifaceted, there is a pressing need for marketers to implement data-driven decision-making to maintain a competitive edge.

Purpose: The primary objective of this research is to examine the impact of marketing analytics on business outcomes, specifically focusing on how companies harness consumer data to craft personalized marketing campaigns and bolster brand loyalty. Additionally, the study explores the transformative role of cutting-edge technologies, including Artificial Intelligence (AI) and Big Data, in redefining traditional marketing strategies.

Methodology: This paper employs a mixed-methods approach, integrating case studies from leading organizations across diverse industries with secondary data analysis. The research examines the efficacy of various marketing analytics tools, such as customer segmentation, predictive modeling, and return on investment (ROI) analysis, while also addressing the ethical considerations tied to data privacy in the analytics process.

Results: The findings reveal that organizations adopting comprehensive marketing analytics strategies can significantly enhance their marketing ROI and customer retention rates. Furthermore, the integration of AI and Big Data enables marketers to

[1] Welingkar Institute of Management Mumbai, India.
E-mail: amandwivedi3702@gmail.com

[2] Welingkar Institute of Management Mumbai, India.
E-mail: shagunrana690@gmail.com

[3] Welingkar Institute of Management Mumbai, India.
E-mail: sahildhalawatjain@gmail.com

achieve greater accuracy in targeting, leading to more effective and personalized campaigns.

Conclusion: Marketing analytics offers substantial advantages by empowering businesses to make informed decisions grounded in consumer insights. However, to harness these benefits fully, organizations must proactively address ethical issues surrounding data privacy and transparency to preserve consumer trust. This study contributes valuable insights for marketing professionals seeking to implement robust analytics frameworks, ultimately guiding them toward more effective strategies in an increasingly data-centric marketplace.

Keywords: *Marketing Analytics, AI, Big Data, ROI, Predictive Modeling, Data Privacy.*

Leveraging Social Media Analytics to Enhance Creative Content Development and Strategy in the Digital Age

Rajpreet Tomar[1], Mansi Bagdai[2] and Aashika Jain[3]

Purpose: The present study aims to examine the role of social media analytics in the creative content development process and the formulation of effective content strategies. As social media continues to shape communication in the digital age, understanding its dynamics has become critical for brands and creators. This research aims to explore the integration of analytics tools into the content creation process, offering a data-driven approach to creativity in the digital landscape.

Methodology: The research follows a mixed-method approach, integrating both qualitative and quantitative data to comprehensively examine the impact of social media analytics on content strategy. The qualitative analysis relies on secondary data sources, including a literature review of academic journals, industry reports (Gartner, Statista, Forrester), case studies of successful brands (e.g., Netflix, Nike, Starbucks), and insights from social media analytics platforms like Sprout Social, Hootsuite, and Brandwatch. This helps in understanding themes, trends, and industry perspectives. Additionally, sentiment analysis using NLP tools (VADER, TextBlob) provides insights into customer feedback, gauging emotional tone and preferences. The quantitative analysis involves primary data collection through a structured survey using a questionnaire with closed-ended Likert scale questions (1 to 5), covering demographics, social media usage, perception of analytics, and its influence on content strategy. A sample size of 300 participants, including marketing professionals, content creators, and brand managers, is chosen using stratified random sampling for statistical validity. Data analysis is conducted using SPSS, employing descriptive statistics, correlation analysis, regression analysis, and hypothesis testing (Chi-square, t-tests) to evaluate the relationship between social media analytics and creative content strategies. This mixed-method approach captures both qualitative insights and

[1] Welingkar Institute of Management Development and Research, Mumbai, India. E-mail: rajpreettomar@gmail.com

[2] Welingkar Institute of Management Development and Research, Mumbai, India. E-mail: mansibagdai@gmail.com

[3] Welingkar Institute of Management Development and Research, Mumbai, India. E-mail: aashikajain83@gmail.com

quantitative evidence, enabling triangulation to validate and explain findings effectively.

Findings: The study reveals that social media analytics transforms creative content development by offering deep insights into audience demographics, behavioral trends, and engagement patterns. Key metrics like click-through rates (CTR) and engagement rates measure content effectiveness, while sentiment analysis ensures alignment with audience sentiment, enhancing emotional resonance. Competitor analysis identifies strategic content gaps, and paid social analytics enables optimized ad spend and predictive insights. Influencer analytics further supports targeted amplification. These analytics-driven strategies not only empower brands to produce more targeted, cost-efficient content but also equip managers with actionable insights to make data-driven decisions that enhance ROI and sustain competitive relevance. This research underscores the pivotal role of advanced analytics in content strategy, suggesting future studies could explore AI-powered predictive analytics to further elevate creative outcomes.

Unique: The unique contribution of this study lies in its comprehensive approach to integrating various social media analytics tools—such as audience insights, sentiment analysis, influencer metrics, and competitor analysis—into the creative content development process. By examining how these analytics can inform strategic decisions, the research highlights a data-driven framework that empowers brands to enhance content creation, optimize ad spend, and drive engagement. The use of mixed-method research, combining qualitative insights from case studies and industry reports with primary data collection through surveys, provides a well-rounded view of the topic. Additionally, the study underscores the potential of future research in AI-powered predictive analytics to further refine creative content strategies, a forward-looking perspective that sets it apart from existing studies.

Keywords: *Click Through Rate, Cost Per Click, Influencer Analytics, Performance Metrics, Sentiment Analysis, Social Media Analytics.*

Variability Driven Consumer Segmentation (VDCS) Framework: A Novel and Dynamic Consumer Segmentation Framework using Real-time Data

Ishaan Kapur[1] and Varsha Jain[2]

This paper presents The Variability Driven Consumer Segmentation (VDCS) Framework as a novel method based on behavioural variability to forecast and improve real-time consumer segmentation. Conventional segmentation techniques usually classify customers on a fixed criteria, therefore ignoring the dynamic changes in consumer behaviour resulting from situational and contextual nudges. VDCS addresses this limitation by employing Shannon's Entropy to quantify and categorise consumer behaviour into high and low entropy groups—High Entropy Persons (HEP) and Low Entropy Persons (LEP). These categories capture both routine and exploratory behaviours, allowing for hyper-personalised engagement strategies that adapt in real time to consumer actions.

The VDCS framework operates across multiple segmentation levels, considering a consumer's life stage, response to external stimuli, and contextual factors, thus enabling a nuanced and dynamic understanding of engagement. By assessing changes in behavioural entropy, VDCS captures subtle shifts in consumer intent, distinguishing between impulsive, exploratory behaviour and more habitual, routine engagement patterns. By matching with real-time interests and demands, this enables companies to dynamically modify marketing strategies, thereby improving consumer contact.

This framework builds on several foundational theories, including Cue Utilisation Theory, Nudge Theory, and Stimulus-Response Theory, to interpret consumer behaviour dynamically. By using Shannon's Entropy to quantify behavioural variability, VDCS categorises consumers based on the unpredictability of their actions—classifying high-entropy consumers as exploratory and low-entropy consumers as routine-driven. This entropy-based segmentation enables real-time adaptation to situational and contextual cues, providing brands with precise, hyper-personalised strategies that reflect both immediate and long-term behavioural patterns, aligning with ethical data practices in modern marketing analytics.

[1] MICA, Ahmedabad, India. E-mail: ishaankapur.24@micamail.in

[2] MICA, Ahmedabad, India. E-mail: varsha.jain@micamail.in

The framework is used for scenarios typical in e-commerce and digital media, where fast adaptation to user behaviour is crucial, therefore highlighting VDCS's practical relevance. Consumers with high entropy during holiday seasons, for example, can be drawn to novelty-oriented marketing, while those with lesser entropy get product recommendations that fit past tastes. By using behavioural data instead of sensitive demographic information, the paper also considers the ethical issues of data usage and privacy. Therefore, it is balancing efficient personalisation with customer data protection.

In conclusion, the VDCS Framework provides a comprehensive, and a flexible model that narrows down a significant segmentation gap by identifying and adjusting to customer behaviour, therefore enabling companies to drive significant, real-time interaction. This method offers a responsible, and technically advanced solution for the field of marketing today since it conforms with modern needs for personalising and ethical data use.

Keywords: *Marketing Analytics, Consumer Segmentation, Dynamic Consumer Profiling, Entropy-based Segmentation, Hyper-personalised Marketing, Consumer Engagement Strategies, Behavioural Insights, Adaptive Marketing Strategy, Data-Driven Personalisation.*

TRACK 4

Marketing Communication and Advertising

Social Media Reels Impacting the Sales of Green Grocers: A Study from Gender Perspective

Ranjit Gadhavi[1] and Aman Dubey[2]

Social media provides a platform to engage and interact with consumers using multiple ways of marketing (Appel *et al.*, 2020). It has been considered a strategic communication tool in times of crisis (Eriksson 2018). Today's consumers dependency on traditional media, such as radio, television, and magazines, is shifting towards the social media sites (Schivinski and Dabrowski 2016). Even the government departments and small businesses are increasingly adopting social media for strategic communication and public relations (Macnamara and Zerfass 2012). An organisation can communicate about their product with millions of young consumers using social media platforms (Duffett 2017). Social media reels consumption has increased with time, and its usage for marketing has seen growth (Sisova 2023). In this empirical study, we explored the impact of social media reels viewed by greengrocers while selling fruits and vegetables in the market. We have conducted semi-structured interviews (n = 30) with the male and female greengrocers of Rajkot city, Gujarat, India. Both genders are included to understand the impact of watching social media reels on sales during business hours. The data sets were analysed thematically using the five steps given by Clark and Braun (Clarke and Braun 2013). We have used the socio-technical system (STS) theory to understand the social and technical factors that influence the consumption of social media reels by greengrocers. The study reveals that short-form video content (reels) on social media leads to decreased customer engagement and reduced sales volumes for male greengrocers. In contrast, female greengrocers, who have more familial responsibilities, exhibit restraint in their smartphone use during business hours, enhancing their focus on sales interactions and maintaining a strong customer base. Male vendors often face debt due to non-payment of loan installments and lower market sales, while female vendors are free from debts as they focus more on selling their goods. The study suggests that social media reels negatively impact male vendors' businesses and create more opportunities

[1] Dr Babasaheb Ambedkar Open University, Ahmedabad, India.
E-mail: ranjit.gadhavi@gmail.com

[2] Guru Gobind Singh Indraprastha University, Delhi, India. E-mail: amandubeyrs@gmail.com

for female vendors, highlighting the need for more effective strategies to support female entrepreneurs. The study also highlights the negative impact of social media engagement on small businesses.

Keywords: *Social Media Reels, Greengrocer, Social Media Engagement, Gender, Small Businesses.*

Brand Profanity: Impact of Euphemistic Swearing on Perceived Hedonism and Brand Preference

Sukriti Sekhri[1] and Tanvi Gupta[2]

Euphemistic-swearing involves an altered spelling of a swear-word to reduce its taboo nature. Through six experiments, this research shows that euphemistic-swearing by brands increases brand preference, mediated by perceived product hedonism and self-brand congruence. This favorable effect of euphemistic-swearing is mitigated among restrained eaters and collectivist regional cultures.

Keywords: *Brand Communication, Brand Profanity, Indulgent Consumption, Experiments.*

[1]SP Jain Institute of Management & Research, Mumbai, India.
E-mail: sukhsekhri@gmail.com

[2]IIM-Ahmedabad, Ahmedabad, India. E-mail: tanvig@iima.ac.in

Connecting Generations, Triggering Emotions: Impact of Nostalgia Marketing on Long-Term Brand Value

Tanmay Aggarwal[1] and Harsh Rajput[2]

Introduction: The research paper explains the rise of nostalgia marketing considering how the era of endless advancements has been particularly appealing to millennials and gen Z alike. Tapping into positive recollections and shared experiences allows brands to reach through the clutter of digital channels and relate with consumers, which helps foster brand and consumer loyalty. The paper also describes how moment marketing, which aims at culturally relevant communication in current times, is also gaining ground as a working strategy.

Literature Review: The literature review studies nostalgia marketing as an integral part of the evolving branding landscape. According to the study, nostalgia fosters emotions of social belonging and psychological resilience by evoking a sense of connection to one's past, particularly during stressful or times of uncertainty. Nostalgia Marketing plays a part in helping customers recall their favourite past interactions with the brand, using phrases, music, celebrities, costumes, or other elements to link the product or service being advertised with these memories, particularly in the audio-visual format of advertising.

Making Use of Nostalgia as a Marketing Strategy: The study demonstrates that nostalgia marketing is effective for all age groups, even though it is generally believed to be a strategy that appeals to older generations. The study claims that marketing campaigns that appeal to nostalgia, such as Nintendo's NES Classic Mini and The Gap's 90s Collection, can significantly increase consumer involvement. It's important to realize that nostalgia marketing doesn't necessarily immediately increase buy intentions; rather, its primary advantages lie in building long-lasting client loyalty and brand identification.

Industry Applications and Case Studies: A table in the document illustrates how various industries, from beverages to media, have leveraged nostalgia marketing. Companies like Coca-Cola, Disney, and Nintendo have successfully rekindled

[1] Welingkar Institute of Management Development and Research, Mumbai, India. E-mail: tanmay.m.agg@gmail.com

[2] Welingkar Institute of Management Development and Research, Mumbai, India. E-mail: harshrajput8871@gmail.com

emotional connections with older consumers while also appealing to newer generations through nostalgic themes. Examples like Disney's live-action remakes, including "The Lion King", demonstrate how nostalgia can appeal to broad audiences.

Nostalgia and Consumer Behaviour: The document highlights the ability of nostalgia to influence consumer behaviour by creating positive emotional associations with a brand. This emotional resonance is particularly strong with older generations, though younger consumers are also increasingly responsive. Brands that balance nostalgic engagement with product relevance, as Ford did with its re-launch of the Bronco, can appeal to a wide demographic.

Research Methodology: The research methodology includes a mixed-methods approach, utilizing both secondary research (academic journals, case studies) and primary research (consumer surveys). The primary research focuses on Millennials and Gen Z, analysing their emotional responses to nostalgia-based advertisements and their subsequent brand loyalty.

Conclusion: The research paper concludes that, while nostalgia marketing is highly effective in creating emotional connections and fostering brand loyalty, it carries certain risks. Brands must balance nostalgic elements with modern relevance to avoid distancing consumers. When used strategically, nostalgia marketing can build long-term emotional bonds, driving brand loyalty and sustained consumer engagement. This research provides valuable insights into the nuanced impact of nostalgia and moment marketing, offering brands recommendations on how to leverage these strategies to foster deep connections with consumers across generations.

Keywords: *Nostalgia Marketing, Consumer Behaviour, Brand Image, Psychological Influence, Storytelling, Retro Branding, Brand Loyalty, Brand Trust, Emotional Resonance.*

Communicating Green: The Key Challenges Marketers Face in Marketing Green Products

Bente Fatema[1]

Marketers present green products to consumers; who then make purchase decisions based on these offerings. Now, if there is a gap between consumer attitude and their actual buying action for green product, both marketers and consumers contribute to this gap. In binary term, this is because either the product is not well marketed, leading to poor awareness and engagement, or the product fails to meet consumer expectations, resulting in a lack of interest or acceptance. While factors that hinder consumers' green product adoption are well-documented in green literature, there is less understanding of the challenges marketers face in marketing these products. Thus, in order to address the green gap more holistically, the present study has endeavored to shed light on the key challenges marketers face in marketing green products.

To achieve this, green marketers were reached out and were asked to reflect on their experiences of working with green brands and identify and elaborate the most common and most prevailing challenges they faced in their green marketing efforts. It was revealed that their biggest challenge comes from the credibility concerns arising from green washing practices. Price-value paradox and sustainability literacy gap of consumers also creates formidable challenge for them in communicating and advertising green products. In addition, drawing from their own experiences, marketers provided recommendation for addressing those daunting disruptions.

Insights into the challenges marketers face in marketing green products and the solutions that can address those challenges hold important significance for both academe and green marketers. By including the voice of marketers in green research trajectory academe will benefit from a novel perspective in green literature. At the same time, for green marketers, these insights will allow them to better align their green marketing efforts with consumer needs and preferences, thus taking a step closer to bridge the gap between consumer attitudes and actual purchasing behaviour.

Keywords: *Sustainable Product, Green Product, Marketing Green Product, Green Marketer, Green Gap.*

---

[1]Queen Mary University of London, London, United Kingdom.
E-mail: bentefatemanaqvi1@gmail.com

[Submission ID 5926 • Track 4]

Can the Media Help Transgender Bias at Work? A Construal Theory Approach

Vineeta Dwivedi[1] and Sunny Arora[2]

Workplace inclusivity, though widely promoted, remains an elusive goal, particularly for transgender individuals who often face bias and discrimination in hiring, promotion, and everyday workplace interactions. Gender, as a complex societal construct and personal identity marker, plays a significant role in shaping these biases. Research has revealed the fluidity and diversity of gender beyond traditional binary perceptions (Hamidi *et al.*, 2018), while transgender individuals resist systems like Automatic Gender Recognition, which rely solely on physical traits. Transgender people, who challenge the notion of fixed, biologically determined gender (Schilt & Westbrook, 2009), continue to face distinct struggles compared to LGB individuals in the workplace (Budge *et al.*, 2010), despite legal advancements such as the 2020 U.S. Supreme Court ruling and India's Transgender Persons Act of 2019 (Morrison, 2022; Zachariah & Nandini, 2023).

This study aims to investigate biases in workplace decision-making related to gender identity, specifically focusing on hiring for senior positions, team selection, and attributing blame in fraud cases. Additionally, it explores the portrayal of transgender individuals in media, often presented through stereotypical and limited narratives (McLaren, 2018), contributing to the reinforcement of heteronormative standards (Glover, 2016). Understanding these biases is critical for fostering a truly inclusive workplace.

Keywords: *Transgender, Media, Construal Theory.*

[1]S.P. Jain Institute of Management & Research, Mumbai, India.
E-mail: vineeta.dwivedi@spjimr.org

[2]S.P. Jain Institute of Management & Research, Mumbai, India.
E-mail: sunny.arora@spjimr.org

Developing a Data-Driven Framework for Creating Emotionally Resonant and Future-Proof Advertisements to Maximize ROI

Suraj Nandi[1]

The study aims to explore the key elements that make advertisements relevant to consumers, both now and in the future. In today's marketing landscape, brands often face the challenge of creating commercials that resonate with their audience. While some advertisements, like the "Imperial Blue" series or the "5 Star Do Nothing" campaign, succeed in capturing attention and generating brand love, many others fail to connect with consumers and result in wasted resources. The absence of a standardized framework for developing relevant and impactful ads further complicates the issue, leading to reduced return on investment (ROI) and diminished brand influence, recall and relatability.

This research will address this challenge by proposing a comprehensive model for brands to create more relevant ads. Using a dataset of approximately 2, 000 award-winning and nominated commercials from India and worldwide across 5 years (2019-23), the study will classify these ads into themes and emotions based on Nielsen's thematic structure and Kantar's needscope six emotive framework. A machine learning model will be developed to scan and classify these ads, identifying patterns between successful commercials and their thematic or emotional constructs. This modelling approach will be further supported by qualitative research to refine the understanding of consumer attitudes toward different advertising styles.

The final output will be a strategic model/framework that enables brands to develop commercials that are aligned with consumer expectations, emotions, and cultural trends. This framework will provide insights into the themes and emotions that drive effective advertising, allowing brands to optimize their ad strategies for better ROI and stronger consumer connections. The study's findings will help bridge the gap in the current advertising landscape by offering a structured approach to creating relevant and future-proof commercials.

Keywords: *Advertisement, Effectiveness, Resonance, Engagement, Return on Investment (ROI), Emotions, Themes, Modelling, Patterns, Classification.*

[1]MICA, Ahmedabad, India. E-mail: surajnandi.23@micamail.in

[Submission ID 6641 • Track 4]

Politics of Gendered Beauty: Misrepresentation(s) in Global Cosmetic Branding: Analysing the Discourses through Feminist and Social Constructivist Approaches

Saurabh Das[1] and Romita Handa[2]

The politicization of gender continues to embrace the beauty standards of India which furthers the positionality of the stereotypes themselves. The brands that soak themselves in consumer fetishism also reveal the vicious loop of a binary understanding of gender that they often mimic and reproduce. Whose identity in this context gets represented becomes an imperative question. We therefore Feminist and Social Constructivist understanding of the construction of narratives by the two popular brands Dove and L'Oreal through a methodological framework of Critical Discourse Analysis. While doing so, we also employ a holistic overview of the varied campaigns and the plausible intervention of AI. Henceforth, the consumer-producer negotiation and the constant role reversal raise significant questions in the neo-liberal and post-capitalistic era. With the intervention of varied realities, the brands thus become incapable of representing the whole, therefore championing a majoritarian perspective, pushing the margins further.

Keywords: *Gendered Beauty, Stereotypes, Artificial Intelligence, Post-capitalism, Post-feminism, Subaltern Discourse.*

[1]Christ University, Bangalore, India. E-mail: saurabh.das1985@gmail.com

[2] Christ University, Bangalore, India. E-mail: romita406@gmail.com

Advertising of CSR Activities and its Impact on Brand Equity: A Study of FMCG Sector in India

Anshul Garg[1], Sarvesh Rahate[2] and Hetali Parmar[3]

Corporate Social Responsibility (CSR) has become an essential component of corporate strategy, with organizations allocating substantial resources to various social and environmental initiatives. This research focuses on examining how the promotion of CSR activities influences brand equity within the Fast-Moving Consumer Goods (FMCG) sector in India. The central hypothesis posits that there is a positive relationship between the marketing of CSR efforts by FMCG companies and their brand equity.

A quantitative research approach was utilized in this study, involving a survey conducted with 155 participants from varied demographic backgrounds. Data were gathered through a structured questionnaire aimed at evaluating participants' awareness of CSR, their responses to CSR advertisements across media platforms, and their perceptions of the brand equity associated with different FMCG brands.

The analysis indicated a modest positive correlation between the advertising of CSR initiatives and brand equity among participants. While consumers demonstrate an appreciation for CSR and its impact on brand loyalty, skepticism regarding authenticity and price sensitivity underscore the necessity for companies to adopt transparent and authentic CSR strategies.

While the findings support a positive link between CSR advertising and brand equity, the future investigations could delve into alternative advertising avenues and examine the long-term effects of CSR initiatives on brand equity. Limitations of this study include its sample size and the potential for self-selection bias among respondents.

Keywords: *CSR, FMCG, Brand Equity, CSR Advertising, Advertising.*

[1] SVKMs, NMIMS, Shobhaben Pratapbhai Patel School of Pharmacy & Technology Management, Mumbai, India. E-mail: Ph.d.anshul@gmail.com

[2] SVKMs, NMIMS, Shobhaben Pratapbhai Patel School of Pharmacy & Technology Management, Mumbai Suburban, India. E-mail: talk2srahate@gmail.com

[3] SVKMs, NMIMS, Shobhaben Pratapbhai Patel School of Pharmacy & Technology Management, Mumbai Suburban, India. E-mail: hetalip2107@gmail.com

[Submission ID 8912 • Track 4]

Influence of AI-Integrated Advertising on Indian Consumers

Siddhi Chauhan[1] and Danika Aggarwal[2]

This study investigates the factors defining the influence of AI-integrated advertising on Indian consumers. With the rapid integration of artificial intelligence (AI) technologies in marketing, understanding consumer responses in emerging markets like India becomes crucial. The research examines Indian consumers' perceptions, attitudes, and behaviours towards AI-driven advertising. Employing a mixed-method approach combining quantitative surveys and qualitative interviews, the study uncovers key factors such as personalisation, privacy concerns, and trust that shape consumer influence. The findings contribute to the academic discourse on AI in advertising and offer practical insights for marketers aiming to optimise AI strategies in the Indian context.

Keywords: *AI-integrated Advertising, Indian Consumers, Consumer Behaviour, Artificial Intelligence, Marketing, Personalisation, Privacy Concerns, Trust.*

[1]MICA, Ahmedabad, India. E-mail: siddhichauhan.24@micamail.in

[2]MICA, Ahmedabad, India. E-mail: danikaaggarwal.24@micamail.in

Synthesizing the Evolution of Green Advertising and Proposing Future Directions

Abhishek[1], Birud Sindhav[2] and Phani Tej Adidam[2]

The field of green advertising originated from environmental advertising, which emerged in response to the rise of green consumerism (Carlson, Grove, and Kangun 1993). While environmental messaging has existed for over a century, it became mainstream in the late 1960s. This shift was driven by growing environmental concerns from scientists, public opinion, and consumers, particularly in response to the environmentally harmful practices of many firms at that time (Easterling, Kenworthy, and Nemzoff 1996).

The 1980s witnessed a sharp increase in the development of green products and advertising. This surge was attributed to a combination of factors: heightened public awareness and concern, increasing competitive pressure among businesses, and the implementation of stricter government regulations related to environmental protection (Carlson, Grove, Laczniak, and Kangun 1996). These developments led to the study of environmental advertising claims, which, due to the growth of green marketing, came to be popularly known as green advertising. The use of the word 'green' in this context was meant to connote pro-environmental behaviors on behalf of both companies and consumers (Iyer 1995).

The most widely adopted definition of green advertising comes from Banerjee, Gulas, and Iyer (1995). They defined it as any advertisement that meets one or more of three criteria: explicitly or implicitly addressing the relationship between a product/service and the biophysical environment, promoting a green lifestyle with or without highlighting a product/service, or presenting a corporate image of environmental responsibility.

In recent years, the United Nations' adoption of 17 Sustainable Development Goals (SDG) as global goals in 2015 has further increased focus on sustainability in business operations. This has led to a surge in research on sustainability in business, particularly in marketing and advertising. Despite this growing body of research,

[1] Institute of Management Technology, India. E-mail: abhishek@imt.edu

[2] University of Nebraska at Omaha, United States. bsindhav@unomaha.edu

[3] University of Nebraska at Omaha, United States. padidam@unomaha.edu

there have been relatively few studies (e.g. Abhishek, Sindhav, Holland, and Adidam, 2022; Agarwal and Kumar, 2021) providing a holistic perspective on green advertising, highlighting the need for a comprehensive review of the field.

This study aimed to synthesize the evolution of green advertising using bibliometric analysis. The researchers collected data from Elsevier's Scopus database using relevant keywords. Initially, 878 documents were identified, which were then reduced to 328 using PRISMA model guidelines. The researchers employed VOSViewer and Biblioshiny, to conduct various analyses, including performance analysis, bibliographic coupling, and keyword analysis.

The study examined documents from 137 sources, spanning from 1993 to 2024, focusing solely on journal articles. A total of 753 authors had contributed to writing 328 documents. On average, there were 2.78 authors per article. Bibliographic coupling analysis revealed eight distinct clusters within the field of green advertising. We are continuing to analyze the clusters for future research directions, and the comparative impact of social media vs. traditional media on green advertising-based brand equity seems to be one of the areas of gap. We should be able to present our full analysis if our abstract is accepted.

Keywords: *Advertising, Green Advertising, Bibliometric Analysis.*

TRACK 5

Artificial Intelligence with Newer Technology

Determining the Well-being of Smart Home Users: A Combination of Value-Added Model and Self-Determination Theory

Megha Agarwal[1], Ajay Kumar[2] and Parvez Ahmad[3]

The widespread proliferation of the Internet and Artificial Intelligence (AI) paved the way for the mass adoption of smart home technologies. Voice assistants are among the most used smart home services. Some voice assistants are Apple's Siri, Amazon's Alexa, Microsoft's Cortana, and Google's Assistant. Voice-assisted speakers use Wi-Fi services to communicate with other devices in your home. This allows smart home speakers to provide voice-activated control and assistance for various devices and services. The global smart home services market has consistently grown since its invention. The notable growth in the smart home speakers market indicates a substantial surge in demand. While numerous studies on adoption have been done, there is a scarcity of research concerning customer experience and well-being post-adoption. This research aims to investigate the factors affecting the well-being of smart home users by considering the value-added model and self-determination theory. The study applied a structured equation modeling (SEM) approach with Smart PLS to test the proposed research hypotheses with collected data (384 responses) through a structured questionnaire. Privacy concerns, personalization, and customer experience values were found to be significant factors affecting smart home users' well-being.

Keywords: *Smart Home Services, Well-being, Self-determination Theory, Value-added Model, Customer Experience.*

[1] School of Management Studies, University of Hyderabad, Hyderabad, India.
E-mail: mittal.megha21@gmail.com

[2] School of Management Studies, University of Hyderabad, Hyderabad, India.
E-mail: ajoykummar24@gmail.com

[3] School of Management Studies, University of Hyderabad, Hyderabad, India.
E-mail: parvezahmed62@gmail.com

[Submission ID 1886 • Track 5]

Analysing the Effect of Artificial Intelligence on Audit Efficiency

Abhishek Bordia[1] and Apeksha Champaneri[2]

This study explores how artificial intelligence (AI) is transforming audit efficiency by automating data analysis, enhancing risk assessment, and enabling real-time monitoring. AI integration allows auditors to streamline operations, reduce human error, and gain deeper insights, significantly boosting financial oversight effectiveness. AI automates data analysis, a traditionally time-consuming and error-prone task. It processes large datasets quickly and accurately, identifying patterns and anomalies that human auditors might miss, thereby accelerating the audit process and ensuring higher accuracy (Brown *et al.*, 2021). Additionally, AI enhances risk assessment through advanced algorithms and machine learning techniques, which evaluate and predict potential risks. By analyzing historical data and current trends, AI forecasts future risks, enabling a proactive approach to risk management and allowing auditors to address issues before they escalate (Smith & Jones, 2022). AI also revolutionizes real-time monitoring. Unlike traditional audits that rely on periodic reviews, AI continuously monitors financial transactions, providing real-time insights. This dynamic and responsive auditing ensures that irregularities are detected and addressed promptly (Williams, 2020). The integration of AI transforms auditors' roles by automating routine tasks, allowing them to focus on strategic activities. This shift enhances financial oversight and increases the value auditors bring to their organizations (Garcia *et al.*, 2023).

Keywords: *Artificial Intelligence (AI), Audit Efficiency, Data Analysis Automation, Risk Assessment, Real-Time Monitoring, Financial Oversight, AI Integration, Accuracy in Auditing, Predictive Algorithms, Machine Learning, Continuous Monitoring, Strategic Auditing, Proactive Risk Management, Auditors' Roles Transformation, Error Reduction.*

[1]RSM, Ahmedabad, India. E-mail: abhishekjain2894@gmail.com

[2] GLS University, Ahmedabad, India. E-mail: apeksha.champaneri@glsuniversity.ac.in

[Submission ID 3525 • Track 5]

A Cross-Cultural Study on the Influence of AI on Language Development among Management Students

A. Dinesh[1] and Samarpita Roy[2]

Language acquisition and usage forms the most important pillar of human development (Global Indian International School, 2024). While it is a known fact that language acquisition is a normal human process that starts early in human life, it is important to observe and discuss how language competencies are developed and propelled throughout human life. Language learning and other competencies among human beings have been transmitted in a physical one-on-one format since time immemorial. However, the advent of technology, especially technologies such as Web 2.0, which started focusing on user-generated content, collaboration, and ease of use, started a new revolution in the process of learning (Kenton, 2024). The development of Generative Artificial Intelligence (AI) has reformed the learning process altogether. Numerous studies suggest that there is a positive correlation between the use of AI and the motivation of students towards learning (Yang, 2024) (Ghafar *et al.*, 2023) (Kaledio, Robert, & Frank, 2024). Further, research has also suggested that AI has a positive impact on AI-assisted learning, thereby navigating towards a self-regulated learning environment (Wei, 2023) (Yang, Li, & Li, 2024). This paper intends to analyse the use of AI in cross-cultural education contexts (America, England, Australia, Canada, Ireland, and other countries) for Language Learning and Development. The paper intends to understand the level of AI integration in such an educational environment and understand the impact of AI technology on specific language skills – listening, speaking, reading and writing (Law, 2024). A survey of international students has been conducted to understand the use of AI in the language learning process. Further, the perceptions of the students have revealed significant information regarding the levels of integration of AI into the system and whether such integration has a positive or a detrimental impact on the overall learning of the students, thus leading to a learning crisis (Charlotte, 2024) (Seo, Tang, Roll, Fels, & Yoon, 2021). This study tries to list a few interesting and engaging AI tools that the students use to improve their listening, speaking, reading, and writing (LSRW) skills. In addition, this study further attempts to find out the most effective AI tools used to improve vocabulary and grammar proficiency from a

[1] Siva Sivani Institute of Management, Hyderabad, India. E-mail: dineshthehuman@gmail.com
[2] Siva Sivani Institute of Management, Hyderabad, India. E-mail: samarpitaroy@ssim.ac.in

cross-cultural perspective. This study also focuses on the perception, attitude, and experience of AI tool/s in cross-cultural students' learning of a language. Further studies need to be conducted to understand the impact of AI on Foreign Language Acquisition (Aijun, 2024). There is also a need to understand the implications of AI on the language use and development of the students, especially with reference to a language already acquired by the students.

Keywords: *Artificial Intelligence, Language Learning, Cross-Cultural Study, Multilingualism, LSRW Skills, Global Learning, Learning and Culture, Learning Crisis.*

Assessing the Impact of Using Generative AI in the Process of Critical Thinking for Strategic Communication

Ruchi Tewari[1], Srushti Govilkar[2] and Priyanshi Jain[3]

Critical thinking is known to be an essential skill in business, a world that is dynamic in nature and facilitates as well as requires problem solving. In order to apply critical thinking in the business world, one needs to have received training in it, which could be done by introducing it in the very beginning of the journey of its employees, i.e., business schools. The pedagogy used to teach critical thinking in B-schools is broadly based on case studies, using business simulations, projects, and group discussions (McEwen, 1994). However, it is a skill which is inherent to strategic thinking as well, which in turn is one of the essential skills for strategic communication (Nuntamanop *et al.*, 2013). The current study explores the impact of using Generative Artificial Intelligence (or GenAI) tools like ChatGPT by students for critical thinking within the context of the course titled - Strategic Communication, which was offered to first year postgraduate students in a business school. Fifty percent of the said course involved using critical and analytical thinking skills to written communication. In order to understand the process of critical thinking, the students were taught different frameworks and were made to practice its application to their writing. Given the emergence of GenAI and its increasing use amongst students worldwide, the students taking the course were encouraged to use it to compare the results they received from it with their own original output and evaluate it against the achievement of the intended goal. This study, thus, collected data from the students via a questionnaire administered in two phases to understand how they use and perceive the output of the GenAI when it comes to higher order thinking like critical thinking and analysis. The results of the first phase revealed that 51% of the students used ChatGPT and 49% did not use it and cited the reason to do so was primarily that they wanted to engage in their own thinking. In the same survey, 82.8% of the students revealed that their critical thinking was superior to that of the ChatGPT. The second phase of the questionnaire was administered a few weeks later, focused on understanding the student's background on the process of critical thinking, experience of using the frameworks and their confidence post the exercise. In doing

[1]MICA, Ahmedabad, India. E-mail: ruchi.tewari@micamail.in

[2]MICA, Ahmedabad, India. E-mail: srushti.govilkar@micamail.in

[3]MICA, Ahmedabad, India. E-mail: priyanshi.jain@micamail.in

so, we aimed to gauge how students interact with curriculum on critical thinking and communication, and the role that is played by the recent rise in GenAI on the same.

Keywords: *Artificial Intelligence, Critical Thinking, Strategic Communication, Strategic Thinking, Pedagogy.*

Unrequited Love: Evaluating the Parasocial Interaction of AI Influencers and Consumer Engagement

Kush Mehta[1] and Varsha Jain[2]

AI influencers, created and managed by artificial intelligence technology, are increasingly being used in global brand marketing campaigns. These digital personas, often in the form of animated characters or avatars, interact with audiences through videos, live streaming, and pre-planned content on social media. They can develop parasocial consumer interactions by simulating human-like characteristics and delivering personalized content, leading to consumer engagement. Generation Z, born between the 1990s and 2010s, is highly likely to engage with AI influencers and develop parasocial interactions. However, there is a gap in academic literature and industry understanding regarding the differential dimensions of AI influencers. This study aims to address the specific characteristics of AI influencers that engage Generation Z consumers and how these engagements might differ from human influencers. The primary research question is:

How do AI influencers, through parasocial interactions, affect consumer engagement among Generation Z consumers? Sub-questions include:

What characteristics of AI influencers foster stronger parasocial interactions with consumers? How do social media post characteristics of AI influencers influence consumer engagement?

The research objectives are to identify and evaluate the factors driving consumer engagement with AI influencers, compare engagement patterns between AI and human influencers among Generation Z consumers, and develop a conceptual framework explaining the relationship between AI influencer characteristics, social media post characteristics, parasocial interaction, and consumer engagement.

This study uses a mixed-method approach, involving qualitative interviews with 40 influencer marketing agencies and a quantitative survey of 400 Gen Z consumers following AI influencers on social media. The research is anchored in parasocial interaction theory and self-determination theory to understand how one-sided relationships between consumers and AI influencers form and how these

[1]MICA, Ahmedabad, India. E-mail: kushmehta778@gmail.com

[2]MICA, Ahmedabad, India. E-mail: varsha.jain@micamail.in

relationships fulfill consumers' psychological needs. The conceptual model consists of AI influencer characteristics (expertise, trustworthiness, social attractiveness, physical attractiveness, and congruence) and social media post characteristics (authenticity, visual appeal, and interactivity) that drive consumer engagement in psychological, behavioral, cognitive, emotional, and co-creational dimensions.

The study proposes that AI influencer characteristics positively influence the development of parasocial interactions with consumers, while social media post characteristics (authenticity, visual appeal, and interactivity) positively influence the development of parasocial interactions. Parasocial interactions mediate the relationship between AI influencer characteristics and consumer engagement, and stronger parasocial interactions lead to higher levels of consumer engagement across psychological, behavioral, cognitive, emotional, and co-creational dimensions.

The research will significantly contribute to the academic literature by extending parasocial interaction theory to the context of AI influencers and integrating self-determination theory to explain how AI influencers satisfy intrinsic psychological needs, contributing to further consumer engagement. The findings will provide valuable data for marketers and brands looking to incorporate AI influencers into their strategies, enabling them to create more successful campaigns, optimize content creation, and select the best AI influencer characteristics and brand collaborations.

Keywords: *AI Influencers, Consumer Engagement, Instagram Marketing, Gen Z Consumers, Parasocial Interaction Theory, Self-Determination Theory.*

[Submission ID 5633 • Track 5]

Revolutionizing Indian Banking: A Deep Dive into Consumer Perspectives and AI Integration: Systematic Literature Review (SLR)

Charmee Shah[1] and Apeksha Champaneri[2]

The goal of this research is to examine prior work on the subject of artificial intelligence (AI) integration in the banking sector of India using a systematic literature review (SLR). Using the PRISMA paradigm, this study examines the industry's and customers' perspectives on how artificial intelligence (AI) is transforming banking services. Chatbots, automated customer care, predictive analytics, and fraud detection are just a few examples of the AI applications that this study synthesizes from a wide variety of academic and business sources to highlight important trends, advantages, and disadvantages. The report emphasizes the increasing value of AI-driven ease, customization, and security, and how these technologies are transforming the user experience. But it does deal with important things like data privacy, ethical concerns, and the digital divide. Through this analysis, the study aims to offer actionable insights into the successful integration of AI, fostering a more adaptive and customer-centric banking environment. Current research predominantly relies on descriptive analysis and secondary data sources. To advance the understanding of consumer perspectives and AI integration in banking, there is a pressing need for empirical research. This study would enrich the existing knowledge base by providing firsthand insights and how AI technologies are influencing consumer behavior and banking practices.

Keywords: *Artificial Intelligence (AI), Banking Sector, Fintech.*

[1] GLS University, Ahmedabad, India. E-mail: charmeesheth@gmail.com

[2] GLS University, Ahmedabad, India. E-mail: apeksha.champaneri@glsuniversity.ac.in

The Future of Digital Marketing in the Era of Artificial Intelligence

Pushpendra Khandelwal[1]

The advent of artificial intelligence (AI) technologies is revolutionizing digital marketing, reshaping how brands engage with consumers, optimize campaigns, and leverage data-driven insights. This comprehensive study explores the multifaceted implications of AI in digital marketing, examining its role in enhancing personalization, automating processes, and driving predictive analytics. By analyzing current trends, industry case studies, and expert insights, this paper elucidates the transformative potential of AI, while addressing ethical considerations and future directions for the field.

Keywords: *Artificial Intelligence (AI), Digital Marketing, Data-Driven Insights, Campaign Optimization.*

[1]XIM University (Bhubaneshwar), Bhubaneshwar, India. E-mail: pushpendra_k@hotmail.com

Negative Effect of AI-mediated Content on Digital Social Consumption

Arnab Pal[1], Rahul Nair[2], Anjali Jain[3], Sameer Patil[4] and Varsha Jain[5]

In the past decade, we have seen rapid growth in Artificial Intelligence & Machine Learning (AI-ML). The newer forms of models (Vaswani, 2017; Ho, 2020) have revolutionized the field of technology and computation. Like every leap in technology, the effect of AI can also be seen in the content landscape. AI is actively affecting how people create and consume content. This interaction and its cascading effect have become an active interdisciplinary area of study by researchers across consumer behaviour, psychology, sociology, communication, technology, etc. In consumer behaviour, where consumer needs and expectations are fast-moving, AI and AI-mediated content have facilitated a faster understanding of them (Edelman & Abraham, 2022). As a result, businesses have rapidly adopted AI for better and quicker segmentation, targeting, and positioning (Jain and Wadhwani *et al.*, 2023). AI is being used to create, curate, modify, and augment interpersonal communication, and this form of communication is termed AI-Mediated Communication (AI-MC) (Mieczkowski *et al.*, 2021). The boundary between man and the machine is disappearing as media has become increasingly interactive, and the underlying technology has started observing, ideating, and proactively interfering with the message (Sundar, 2020). It becomes even more important to delve into the effect AI-MC can have on consumers and their consumption.

This article proposes a conceptual model of how interaction with AI-MC shapes us. We have synthesized multiple established theoretical models from consumer behaviour, psychology, sociology, and technology in the context of AIMC. The proposed model is cyclical and begins when a consumer comes across AIMC. The content they get exposed to can have multiple concurrent media forms—text, audio, video, etc. Multimedia content is information-rich and profoundly impacts the consumer—which we address through further components in the model. The

[1] MICA, Ahmedabad, India. E-mail: arnabpal.24@micamail.in

[2] MICA, Ahmedabad, India. E-mail: rahulnair.24@micamail.in

[3] MICA, Ahmedabad, India. E-mail: anjalijain.24@micamail.in

[4] MICA, Ahmedabad, India. E-mail: sameerpatil.24@micamail.in

[5] MICA, Ahmedabad, India. E-mail: varsha.jain@micamail.in

moment the consumer meets the AI through the AIMC is defined as an interaction. The interaction results in a cascade of effects on the consumer, which can be labelled as experience. The experience that arises from this interaction determines the trustworthiness of the content and, by extension, the creator and includes the consumer anthropomorphising the creator of the content based on the material and information from the content, which is done by imposing human attributes on the content provider. Wan and Chen (2021) talk about three domains of anthropomorphism in shaping object attachment—pleasantness, self-identity, and self-efficacy. Anthropomorphising a piece of communication increases the content's trust, value and engagement. A higher engagement leads to positive emotion and a rise in content consumption. Thus, if its content passes the test of anthropomorphism, the AI sees increased traction and creates more content with the same characteristics, therefore beginning the circle again. However, the circle can get hampered when the anthropomorphism test passes through the uncanny valley. Entities exhibiting human-like shapes and behaviour, such as humanoid robots and computer-animated characters, are often regarded more favourably as their resemblance to humans increases up to a specific threshold (Igaue and Hayashi, 2023). Nevertheless, if such avatars appear nearly, but not quite, human-like, onlookers experience discomfort. The sensation of unease regarding a humanoid figure is called the uncanny valley effect. When content falls into the uncanny valley, it generates negative consumer engagement and emotions.

Successful circles cause the removal of any imperfections. As a result, the contents become more and more flawless, taking it beyond the reach of the ordinary.

Keywords: *AI-ML, Consumer Behaviour, AI-mediated Communication (AIMC), Anthropomorphisation, Uncanny Valley, Engagement.*

Nudged by Algorithms: The Dual Role of Recommender Systems in App Subscription

Tushita Chadha[1]

Music streaming apps' reliance on RS for personalization of playlists is crucial for its freemium model. This research explores how non-subscribers and new subscribers interact with the recommendation algorithms of Music streaming apps, and specifically how the platform makes use of recommendations to encourage upgrades in plans. By employing semiotic analysis for a music streaming app's interface and conducting semi-structured interviews with users—80% of whom are non-subscribers and 20% are recent subscribers—this study aims to explore the interplay between user behavior and the design of the platform. Grounded in Domestication theory, this research explores how users integrate music streaming apps' algorithmic features in daily lives, uncovering underlying motivations that drive recent subscribers to upgrade and the challenges faced by non-subscribers. Findings of the study suggest that recommendations from the platform are crucial in shaping experiences of the users while reinforcing commercial objectives of the freemium model. This study contributes to the understanding how algorithm-driven systems like music streaming apps' domesticate the users, in turn influencing their engagement patterns and subscription decisions.

Keywords: *Music Streaming, Algorithmic Domestication, Intention to Subscribe, Semiotic Analysis.*

[1] International Management Institute, New Delhi, India. E-mail: tushita.f21@imi.edu

Dark Sides of Conversational Artificial Intelligence and its Effect on Consumer Experience

Divyanshu Kumar[1], Parth Salunke[2] and Varsha Jain[3]

Conversational Artificial Intelligence (CAI) systems, including chatbots and virtual assistants, shape how customers engage with service providers. These systems are increasingly integrated into customer-AI interactions across industries, bringing much-needed operational efficiency. However, several challenges have been related to privacy concerns, algorithmic biases, and emotional disconnect during customer interactions. These concerns, which may serve as the dark side of AI, often affect the overall consumer experience. Reliance on AI-driven services has been ever-increasing, and thus, the concerns about data privacy, security, and emotional disconnects have intensified. Industry reports by Capgemini (2019) found that 62% of consumers express trust issues with how AI systems handle user data. Deloitte (2024) also stated that around 58% of consumers feel uneasy about how AI collects and stores their information. Such systems may often embrace gender, racial, and socio-economic biases, leading to inequitable treatment of certain demographic groups (Pelau *et al.*, 2021) across industries. These dark sides become even more relevant in industries where customer trust is crucial, such as banking and finance. PwC (2023) found that 74% of banking customers still prefer human interaction for complex issues, underscoring the limitations of CAI in providing appropriate solutions and reassurance for fraud inquiries, loan rejections, etc. Therefore, failure to meet such expectations for human-like interaction, especially in high-stakes environments, can affect consumer experiences. However, studies in the literature on conversational AI are limited, and more in-depth exploration of the dark sides of conversational AI and its effect on consumer experiences is needed.

This study aims to understand and explore the dark sides of CAI and how and why it affects overall consumer experiences. Thus, we use the Uncanny Valley (Mohri, 1970) theory to understand the dark sides of AI that build discomfort among consumers and affect their experiences. Expectation-Confirmation Theory (ECT) (Oliver, 1980) is utilized to know how unmet customer expectations—particularly

[1] MICA, Ahmedabad, India. E-mail: divyanshukumar.23@micamail.in
[2] MICA, Ahmedabad, India. E-mail: parthsalunke.fpm21@micamail.in
[3] MICA, Ahmedabad, India. E-mail: varsha.jain@micamail.in

regarding privacy, fairness, and emotional engagement—lead to customer dissatisfaction. This study adopts a mixed-methods approach to examine the core RQs, focusing specifically on the Banking and Financial Services Industry (BFSI). The BFSI sector is chosen for its heavy reliance on AI-driven interactions to handle sensitive data, where trust and security are paramount. Given the industry's increasing integration of conversational AI, BFSI provides a critical context for examining the effects of the above-hypothesized challenges on the overall consumer experience, and research intends to make valuable contributions to academia, industry, and society. Academically, it deepens the theoretical understanding of human-AI interaction and opens new avenues for future research, primarily in consumer experience. For industry professionals, the study offers practical insights that can help organisations optimise the implementation and development of CAI systems. By mitigating factors that negatively affect consumer experience, businesses save costs and improve overall efficiency. Finally, this research contributes to the broader societal discourse on ethical AI deployment, emphasizing the need for responsible AI governance and practices to protect privacy, promote equity, and build long-term trust with end users.

Keywords: *Conversational Artificial Intelligence, Customer Experience, Trust, Satisfaction, Emotional Disconnect, Data Security, Privacy Concerns, Algorithmic Bias, Automation Bias, BFSI.*

Cross-User Recommendation Systems: Redefining Personalization in Multi-User Scenarios by Leveraging Collaborative Behavioral Data

Yash Gupta[1] and Divyanshu Kumar[2]

Recommendation systems have revolutionized various industries, including e-commerce, social media, and entertainment platforms, by offering personalized suggestions that improve user engagement and satisfaction. Current systems primarily focus on individual preferences, which is highly effective but limited in scenarios like gift-giving, team collaboration, and family-oriented decisions, where recommendations must cater to someone other than the primary user. Research has shown that over 60% of consumers struggle with selecting gifts, highlighting the gaps in traditional recommendation engines (Zebra Technologies, 2022). Furthermore, with consumers increasingly demanding hyper-personalization, recommendation systems need to adapt by incorporating data from multiple users, thus giving rise to cross-user recommendation systems.

This research addresses the limitations of traditional single-user models by proposing a cross-user recommendation system. Such a system incorporates both the giver's and the recipient's preferences, allowing for more accurate and contextually relevant recommendations. Current systems, while powerful, do not fully account for the social and emotional complexities involved in selecting products for others. The proposed cross-user system addresses this by leveraging hybrid models of collaborative filtering and content-based filtering, enriched by persona clustering and contextual data such as relationship dynamics and the occasion for gift-giving.

Existing literature has explored collaborative filtering (Sarwar *et al.*, 2001) and content-based filtering (Lops *et al.*, 2011), but these approaches are limited in cross-user contexts. The application of hybrid models (Zhang *et al.*, 2019) has been promising, combining user behaviors and item characteristics. Still, the unique challenges of recommending for one person based on another's preferences remain underexplored. Studies on gift-giving highlight the emotional and social importance of such systems, showing that intent-based recommendations improve user

[1] MICA, Ahmedabad, India. E-mail: yashgupta.23@micamail.in
[2] MICA, Ahmedabad, India. E-mail: divyanshukumar.23@micamail.in

satisfaction (Mohseni *et al.*, 2023). This system also addresses data privacy concerns by utilizing privacy-preserving mechanisms, an increasingly critical consideration in handling cross-user data (Kim *et al.*, 2011).

The theoretical framework builds on traditional collaborative filtering but extends it by incorporating multiple user profiles and persona clustering. Matrix factorization techniques are adapted to analyze shared preferences and interactions between users, offering more informed recommendations. This hybrid model allows for greater personalization by considering both the giver's and the recipient's behavioral data.

The research questions focus on improving personalization for third parties, such as gift recipients, and assessing the benefits and challenges of implementing cross-user systems across different domains like corporate decision-making and family services. The proposed methodology includes collecting data from both gift-givers and recipients and using machine learning models to handle multi-user inputs. Clustering algorithms will further refine the recommendations by grouping users with similar preferences.

The implications of cross-user recommendation systems are profound, offering significant contributions to academia and industry. These systems have the potential to enhance customer satisfaction in e-commerce and corporate environments, foster deeper social connections, and extend their applications to areas like healthcare. The system also holds promise for reducing decision fatigue by making complex, multi-user decisions more manageable.

Keywords: *Cross-user Recommendation Systems, Collaborative Filtering, Content-based Filtering, Persona Clustering, Hybrid Recommendation Model, Artificial Intelligence, Gifting Recommendation.*

[Submission ID 9065 • Track 5]

Exploring Mainstream Users' Perspectives on ChatGPT and Student's Continued Intention to Use ChatGPT

Rajesh Nadiminti[1], Shweta Dhumal[2], Muskan Madaan[3], Rooshabh Mehta[4] and Krunal Nakrani[5]

AI is increasingly becoming a vital tool for students, helping them improve their learning experiences in multiple ways. Recent statistics reveal that 90% of students who used AI-powered tools like ChatGPT found them more effective than traditional tutoring (MSPowerUser.). In 2023, over 61% of US college students acknowledged that AI will soon be a norm in education, even though many express concerns about ethical usage (MSPowerUser.). The global AI education market is projected to grow significantly, reaching an estimated $80 billion by 2030, further solidifying its role in modern learning (MSPowerUser.).

In this buzz of AI, and its potential benefits, with aided disadvantage or potential threats, research cross the globe are carrying out studies to chronicling the myriad ways AI is being consumed for societal good/bad. Here, the aim of the study is little bit narrow by keeping the focus on AI consumption by students.

As a part of theoretical framework, UTAUT model framework has been selected based on the available literature. The review synthesizes existing research on factors like "Performance Expectancy, Social Influence, Effort Expectancy, Facilitating Conditions, and User Satisfaction". The aim of my research is to explore how these factors influence students' continued intention to use AI tools like ChatGPT for academic purposes. The research sample's size is 414 (participants), specifically targeting students who actively use AI tools like ChatGPT for academic purposes. These participants were chosen to provide a diverse yet representative sample of students who interact with AI for learning, covering a range of educational backgrounds and usage behaviors. The analysis highlights that students who perceive ChatGPT as effective for tasks and experience positive social influence from peers are more likely to keep using it. Additionally, findings based on the statistical analysis

[1]Niper, Ahmedabad, India. E-mail: rajesh.nadiminti@niperahm.res.in

[2]Niper, Ahmedabad, India. E-mail: shweta.nipera2325@gmail.com

[3]Niper, Ahmedabad, India. E-mail: muskan.nipera2325@gmail.com

[4]Niper, Ahmedabad, India. E-mail: rooshabh61288@outlook.com

[5]Niper, Ahmedabad, India. E-mail: krunal.niper2224@gmail.com

suggest that students find using ChatGPT enjoyable, which significantly contributes to its seamless integration into their daily academic routines. Interestingly, the perceived ease of use and availability of support appear less critical for continued engagement, suggesting an inherent user-friendliness of ChatGPT. This review sheds light on the factors that captivate students and paves the way for further exploration of the long-term impact of language models like ChatGPT on education.

Keywords: *ChatGPT, Continued Intention, Performance Expectancy, Effort Expectancy, Social Influence, Facilitating Condition, User Satisfaction, UTAUT Model.*

Posts, Privacy and Plight: Investigating Ethical Boundaries of Consumer Data Usage

Sanjuktha Vikram[1] and Khyati Jagani[2]

The swift digitisation of society and the widespread use of Artificial Intelligence (AI) technologies have presented fresh obstacles to data security and privacy, especially with the employment of user-generated information on social media platforms. This study looks at privacy regarding privacy policy modifications, which permit the company to train its AI models using publicly uploaded photos, videos, and other information on social media. This study investigates the concerns of young consumers in India regarding these social media policy change and their perceptions of data security and platform trust. This exploratory study uses semi-structured, in-depth interviews to understand the perspectives of users who manage public accounts on consent, transparency, and striking a balance between AI innovation and consumer privacy. The results will provide important context for understanding how this segment negotiates with privacy issues and whether they support or oppose using their public information for AI training. The findings will add to the ongoing conversation on moral AI procedures and the value of privacy in the digital era.

Keywords: *Artificial Intelligence, Privacy Concerns, Ethical AI, Social Media.*

[1] FLAME University, Pune, India. E-mail: sanjuktha.vikram@flame.edu.in

[2] FLAME University, Pune, India. E-mail: khyati.jagani@flame.edu.in

TRACK 6

Branding in the Digital Age

Branding in the Digital Age: The Impact of Narrative and Storytelling on Consumer Engagement

Naisha Patel[1] and T.K. Krishnapriya[2]

Background: In the era of digital age, brands must build a narrative to hook and hold consumer engagement, effectively publishing their identity in an oversaturated market. The famous 'Just Do It' campaign by Nike is a textbook example of exhibiting brand identity via storytelling. Coca-Cola's campaigns, such as 'Share the Happiness', reclaimed the brand's position as a source of joy by evoking camaraderie via clever narratives. However, if not created with due consideration of the socio-cultural environment, it can backfire. Pepsi encountered immense criticism when its storytelling narrative offended socially and politically marginalised sections.

Digital-first lifestyle brands look at digital platforms to do commerce and conduct consumer engagement, lifestyle covering a sea of products and services that enable consumers attain a way of living through their products, verifying desired identities and promoting a sense of community.

Objective: This study looks at how brands utilise storytelling to improve consumer engagement and loyalty in the digital age. It also examines how digital-first lifestyle brands double down on storytelling to better their market positioning. The research seeks to show how such narrative marketing influences consumer perceptions and choices.

Methods: The paper will adopt a case study approach combining qualitative and quantitative methods to explore the storytelling strategies of digital-first lifestyle brands - The Plated Project, Masaba, Emirates, and Airbnb. These brands showcase various narrative styles since they belong to different segments of the market, they enable cross-industry and audience comparison, displaying a range of storytelling practices. Authenticity, emotional resonance, and cultural relevance will be poles of discussion in dissecting and analysing their strategies.

Further, the study will utilise the theoretical framework adopted from Narrative Transportation Theory, which explains how consumers get immersed in a narrative,

[1] Christ University, Bangalore, India. E-mail: naisha.patel@emp.christuniversity.in

[2] Christ University, Bangalore, India. E-mail: krishnapriya.tk@christuniversity.in

affecting their choices and decision-making, and Archetypal Branding Theory, which employs universal templates to create emotionally resonant and culturally relevant brand narratives.

The selected brands utilise multiple communication methods keeping in mind their target demographics. Social Cause, Cultural Richness, Luxury, and Global Belonging are critical elements of their brand narratives. This study will be studying the key themes, narrative structures and other aspects to understand its marketing approach.

Scope of the Study: This research will explore the power of storytelling in shaping and managing brand perception. Existing literature reveals that effective brand storytelling uses stories that are authentic and can resonate with customers, being culturally relevant to the target market. In the age of algorithms, this research can show brands how utilising effective storytelling techniques can benefit their brand positioning.

Justification for the Study: This study aims to look at the influence storytelling has on brands image, studying how marketing impactful narratives are translated from mere product promotion to foster connections via experiences. Further, it will examine how the use of authentic narratives can help brands adopt strategies that resonate with audiences and grip loyalty. This research will explore storytelling techniques that have provided results in the digital age, enabling organisations to leverage narratives to claim their market position.

Keywords: *Storytelling, Consumer Engagement, Digital First Brands, Brand Narratives, Narrative-driven Marketing, Lifestyle Brands, Narrative Transportation Theory, Archetypal Branding Theory.*

[Submission ID 5146 • Track 6]

Leveraging NFT Blockchain for Enhanced Customer Engagement in the Digital Fashion Landscape: A New Era of Marketing Innovation

Sachin Kaushik[1]

The rise of blockchain technologies and Non-Fungible Tokens (NFTs) in the digital fashion landscape presents unprecedented opportunities for brand engagement and narrative building. However, the integration of these technologies into the fashion ecosystem is still nascent, with limited studies investigating their true impact on consumer behavior, brand loyalty, and storytelling. This paper explores how NFTs are reshaping customer engagement in fashion, while addressing key gaps in existing research, particularly around the scalability of NFT adoption, the intersection of NFT technology with sustainability goals, and the long-term impact on brand perception. A mixed-methods approach reveals that while NFTs hold potential for reshaping brand-consumer dynamics, several obstacles prevent their widespread adoption. We propose a framework for understanding these challenges and how brands can overcome them.

Keywords: *NFTs, Blockchain, Digital Fashion, Customer Engagement, Brand Narratives, Marketing Innovation.*

[1]MICA, Ahmedabad, India. E-mail: sachinkaushik.24@micamail.in

Gendered Branding: Examining the Relationship between Masculinity, Femininity, and Brand Choice

Prerna Dongre[1] and Sajith Narayanan[2]

This research delves into the intricate relationship between individual personality attributes and brand choice, with a focus on the influence of congruence between personality attributes of individuals and brands on consumer outcomes. Employing a quantitative approach and validated scales, the study investigates purchase intention, brand love, and perceived quality across two product categories: soft drinks and packaged drinking water. Findings reveal significant effects of congruence on consumer behaviour, emphasising the significance of aligning brand's gender attributes with self-concept of the customer. This study contributes valuable insights for marketers aiming to enhance brand-consumer relationships and drive positive consumer outcomes. The implications extend to both academic scholarship and practical applications in marketing and brand management, highlighting avenues for future research to deepen our understanding of brand-consumer dynamics.

Keywords: *Masculinity, Femininity, Brand Personality, Congruence, Purchase Intention, Brand Love.*

[1] DDB Mudra Group, Mumbai, India. E-mail: prernadongre66@gmail.com

[2] FLAME University, Pune, India. E-mail: sajith.narayanan@flame.edu.in

[Submission ID 6539 • Track 6]

Entrepreneurial Failure: The Case of Impression Mismanagement

Ashapurna Das[1] and Apurva Sanaria[2]

Entrepreneurial failure, especially in the social domain, is extremely challenging because social setbacks involve interactions with others, who may not be easily persuaded or influenced. Impression management literature has so far focused on the successful delivery of impressions, while poorly executed impressions and their aftermath have rarely received scholarly attention. Our paper aims to advance this scholarly discourse by advocating the need to efficiently recover after a mismanaged impression in the context of entrepreneurship. We are particularly interested in studying this phenomenon in the context of pitch competitions where impression stakes are higher. Recovery from failed impression management is important because it facilitates the restoration of vital resources for purposive action, preparing an entrepreneur for their next pitch. Our primary research question is: How can entrepreneurs efficiently recover from instances of impression mismanagement experienced at pitch competitions? We explore this by advancing Shepherd's (2003) work on entrepreneurial grief recovery.

Keywords: *Entrepreneurs, Impression Mismanagement, Recovery, Pitch Competitions.*

[1]Indian Institute of Management Bangalore (IIMB), Bangalore, India.
E-mail: ashapurna.das24@iimb.ac.in

[2]Indian Institute of Management Bangalore (IIMB), Bangalore, India.
E-mail: apurva.sanaria@gmail.com

Spiritual Branding: An Analysis of Instagram Reels of Indian Spiritual Organisations

Titas Bandyopadhyay[1], Madhu Veechika Kuppa[2] and Soumyadeep Bandyopadhyay[3]

Spirituality in India has evolved from a deeply personal practice into a highly digitised tool for "mindful living" and "balanced lifestyle". India is often regarded as the hub of Spiritual Capital, holding one of the largest global markets for spiritual practices with organisations like Isha Foundation and Art of Living Foundation architecting the living rooms of individuals invading personal spirituality with technological tools. These two brands were chosen after evaluating the statistics from popular spiritual organisations in India. The paper examines the digital identities of these organisations, applying content, textual and discourse analysis of their Instagram reels. In the digital age, branding of spiritual organisations has evolved into inviting a consumer market that is highly competent with commercial goods market. Traditional markets often focus on commercial sectors; spiritual markets are mission-driven and non-profit. Observing contemporary Services and Products that spiritual organisations offer, these two are no longer separate roads diverging as Materialism and Spiritualism for an individual. Spiritual Brands now compete with materialism-inducing brands, leading to a constant online presence through app pop-ups or notification alerts, sponsored content, influencer marketing strategies, and everything that traditional commercial market practices. This faith washes their "Profituality" dimension of the spiritual organisation.

Our study is built on the technological determinist perspective. Drawing upon Katz and Blumer's Uses and Gratifications theory, the study interprets how these organisations meet their audience's psychological and social needs through their online marketing strategies.

Methodology: The study focuses on establishing the most preferred social media content that users like to engage with through a survey, i.e., Instagram reels, and understanding the spiritual organisations' digital identity based on the followers, likes, comments and shares, impact through the comments and activity presence

[1]Indian Institute of Technology, Guwahati, India. E-mail: b.titas@iitg.ac.in

[2]Indian Institute of Technology, Guwahati, India. E-mail: m.kuppa@iitg.ac.in

[3]XLRI, Jamshedpur, India. E-mail: fh20005@astra.xlri.ac.in

through the frequency of reels. Specifically, our concept of digital identity for Spiritual brands is addressed through the following questions: 1. What message do these videos convey? 2. Who is the target audience? 3. What impact do these messages have? 4. What are their Insta reel appeals? 5. How do design elements such as colour schemes, typography, layout, and hashtags contribute to their branding online? 6. What is the audience's response, primarily focusing on their engagement? 7. Does the content follow a particular thematic classification, and if it does, what popular categories do they belong to?

The paper analyses the branding strategy of the spiritual commodification of non-profit spiritual organisations. Adopting content, discourse, and textual analysis methods, the paper studies the Instagram reels of the two brands that were produced in three months.

Significance: The selected organisations mainly employ strategies like cross-cultural branding, the intersection of tradition and modernity, and enforcing the application of Indian Knowledge Systems in the everyday practices of users. It digs into the usage of non-profit branding and how these strategies build the umbrella of faith, loyalty and "spirituality" as well as "profituality" as their brand identity and engage in value-laden communication without appearing overly commercial. The study further explores the analysis of Experiential Branding in a Spiritual Context in the future research scope.

Keywords: *Spirituality, Instagram Reels, Non-Profit, Social Media, Branding.*

TRACK 7

B2B Marketing and Supply Chain Management in the New Age of Digitization

Creativity in Context: The Impact of Cultural Rigidity on Creative Performance

Ashapurna Das[1] and Apurva Sanaria[2]

Culture plays a fundamental role in human life (Lubart, 2010), influencing many aspects of our lifestyle and identity, including creativity. Different cultures can either foster or hinder conditions that are conducive to creative performance (Niu & Sternberg, 2002), which explains why some cultures exhibit higher levels of creativity than others. This relationship suggests the impact of culture on the two key components of creativity: originality and appropriateness. We highlight the prominent role of cultural rules and norms in the meta-analysis conducted by Barth & Stadtmann (2024) on cross-cultural creativity. While their analysis simply highlighted how different cultures perform creatively, the recurring theme of cultural rules and norms was evident. Building on this, we argue in this paper that the rigidity of a culture affects both the appropriateness and originality of creative expression. We present three propositions that identify how cultural rigidity impacts these components both together and separately. In doing so, we also identify the limiting and facilitating nature of rules and norms in creative performance.

***Keywords:** Cultural Creativity, Cultural Rigidity; Appropriateness, Originality.*

[1] Indian Institute of Management Bangalore (IIMB), Bangalore, India.
E-mail: ashapurna.das24@iimb.ac.in

[2] Indian Institute of Management Bangalore (IIMB), Bangalore, India.
E-mail: apurva.sanaria@gmail.com

TRACK 8

Marketing with Augmented Reality, Mixed Reality, Augmented Reality, Extended Reality and Metaverse

Strategic Adoption of Augmented and Virtual Reality Innovations in Digital Marketing

Sonali A. Abrol[1], Sarah J. Kelly[2] and P. Monica Chien[3]

This paper explores the strategic adoption of augmented and virtual reality (AR/VR) technologies in digital marketing within the post-COVID competitive landscape. AR/VR offers immersive, real-time brand experiences that enhance customer interaction and strengthen brand equity. Despite the significance, many firms are still in the early stages of adopting AR/VR for innovative marketing strategies. Academic Research mainly focuses on AR/VR innovation adoption from consumer lense, while research from firm-centric managerial perspectives is scarce. This study explores the antecedent drivers and barriers that influence the strategic adoption of AR/VR innovations in digital marketing from a managerial standpoint.

By integrating theories from strategic marketing and innovation adoption, this paper extends the Technology-Organization-Environment (TOE) framework by incorporating a strategic dimension to account for brand strategy and temporal planning. The strategic factors are drawn from the Brand Equity theory and Temporal strategy planning framework. We argue that AR/VR innovation benefits evolve over time and the adoption must align with the overall brand strategy, rather than a tactical tool used in isolation.

The research methodology involves a qualitative Theories-in-use approach using semi-structured interviews with 15 global brand marketing professionals who specialize in AR/VR marketing. Interviews are thematically analyzed using NVivo-12 software. The study aims to provide both theoretical insights and practical decision-making tools for managers, enabling them to strategically adopt AR/VR innovations in line with their short- and long-term brand strategies. Data collection will be completed by October 2024, with findings presented at forthcoming conferences.

Keywords: *Digital Marketing, Innovation Adoption, Augmented Reality, Virtual Reality, Strategic Management, Brand Equity.*

[1]The Univesity of Queensland Business School, Australia. E-mail: sonali.11abrol@gmail.com

[2]The Univesity of Queensland Business School, Queensland University of Technology, Australia. E-mail: s.kelly@business.uq.edu.au

[3]The Univesity of Queensland Business School, Australia. E-mail: m.chien@uq.edu.au

Better Customer Experience Guaranteed with AR, MR, and XR in the Metaverse Era

Ayush Sharma[1] and Kaustubh Patil[2]

The rise of cutting-edge technologies like Augmented Reality (AR), Mixed Reality (MR), Extended Reality (XR) and the Metaverse has changed the marketing perspective. The beauty of these platforms is the way customers get experience which is unique in every sense. The amalgamation of these platforms has taken marketing onto a different level of "Customers First Approach". These technologies actually help brands to create more personalised campaigns.

Off-late we have seen many applications of AR, MR, XR in various industries like real estate, education and entertainment. The classic example of AR is Lenskart Virtual-try-on where user can try glasses which gives the sense of real-time experience for the user, whereas Tata Motors had introduced the Mixed Reality solution for customers to visualize the car models and interact with real-world showrooms which some device and lastly Zee5 created an Extended Reality experience where user could watch content in a virtual environment. All these examples demonstrate how brands have given immersive experiences to their customers.

On the other hand, Metaverse is not just the buzz word but it can certainly expand the possibilities for marketers by creating virtual spaces for customer engagement, product launches or branding. For the MICE of the events industry, Metaverse is a boon to have better accessibility and engagement of the participants. It has the solid foundational support of AR, VR and XR along with blockchain and can support the virtual economies. With certain challenges such as high development costs, data privacy etc., it will overcome this and have a better future ahead.

The potential of these marketing strategies extend beyond certain industries. The solid advantage is the ability to bridge the geographical and physical constraints, making the marketing activities scalable. Time has proved that these technologies empower a marketeer to craft personalised communications to the target audience. With the evolution of these technologies, we have seen better customer relationships, enhanced trust and increased transparency. In the cut-throat competition era, when

[1]Jaipuria Institute of Management, Noida, India. E-mail: ayush.sharma.fpm24n@jaipuria.ac.in
[2]Jaipuria Institute of Management, Noida, India. E-mail: kaustubh.patil.fpm24i@jaipuria.ac.in

brands are under immense pressure to differentiate themselves and stay relevant. These technologies provide the competitive edge, foster deep customer loyalty amidst the crowded marketplace.

With the evolution of Industry 5.0, artificial intelligence, machine learning, etc. where customers are very knowledgeable and have more options to buy products/services. Therefore, cutting-edge tools like AR, VR, MR, XR and Metaverse have that ability to ensure that they can guide customers for better informed decisions so that there is a high degree of customer satisfaction and repeat purchase. No doubt that these evolving marketing technologies are the game changer for the industries and they should use them with the caution of following the ethical practices. Thus, having integration of these tools into the Marketing strategy brings a lot of opportunities for brands to connect with the customers regularly in a more interesting manner and it will only rise with the innovative techniques and creative ability of the marketers.

Keywords: *Augmented Reality, Mixed Reality, Extended Reality, Metaverse, Immersive Technologies, Virtual Shopping, Brand Engagement.*

Impact of AR and VR Technologies on Consumer Adoption in the Indian Fashion Industry

Krishna Vyas[1] and Tulsi Raval[2]

Background: The fashion industry is rapidly evolving with the integration of Augmented Reality (AR) and Virtual Reality (VR), transforming consumer interactions and shopping experiences. Despite the potential advantages of these technologies, there is a limited understanding of customer awareness, perceptions, and the factors influencing their adoption within the Indian context.

Objectives: This study aims to:

1. Evaluate the impact of performance expectancy, effort expectancy, social influence, and facilitating conditions on consumer adoption of AR and VR technologies in the fashion industry.
2. Assess consumer awareness and familiarity with AR and VR technologies in the context of fashion shopping among Indian consumers.
3. Analyze the relationship between key determinants and consumers' behavioral intentions to adopt AR and VR technologies.
4. Identify barriers to adoption and provide strategic recommendations for fashion retailers to enhance consumer engagement.

Sampling: A purposive sampling method will be used to collect data from consumers aged 18 and above who have experienced AR or VR technologies while shopping for fashion items. The target sample size is approximately 300 respondents, ensuring diverse representation across demographic categories such as age, gender, education, and income. Data will be collected through an online survey distributed via social media and relevant online fashion communities.

Methodology: The research will employ a structured questionnaire based on the Unified Theory of Acceptance and Use of Technology (UTAUT) model. The questionnaire will include closed-ended questions to evaluate various constructs related to consumer perceptions of AR and VR technologies, including their usefulness, ease of use, social influences, and behavioral intentions. The data collection period will span four weeks.

[1] RK University, Rajkot, India. E-mail: vyas.krishnaphd@gmail.com

[2] SMT. K.S.N. Kansagara Mahila College, Rajkot, India. E-mail: tulsiraval.84@gmail.com

Analysis: Quantitative data will be analyzed using statistical software. Descriptive statistics will summarize demographic information, while multiple regression analysis will be utilized to assess the impact of the independent variables (performance expectancy, effort expectancy, social influence, and facilitating conditions) on the dependent variable (behavioral intention to adopt AR and VR technologies).

Keywords: *Augmented Reality (AR), Virtual Reality (VR), Consumer Adoption, Fashion Industry, Behavioral Intentions, Performance Expectancy, Effort Expectancy, Social Influence, Facilitating Conditions, Consumer Awareness.*

[Submission ID 4720 • Track 8]

A Study on Digital Marketing Strategies in the Retail Sector with Emphasis on Extended Reality and Metaverse

Lakshay Gupta[1], Rajni Kant Singh[2] and Monika Agarwal[3]

This paper delves into the transformative potential of Extended Reality and the Metaverse in contemporary marketing strategies. It introduces the BICK FOUR framework branding, inspiring, convincing, and keeping as a structured approach for organizations to align their marketing goals with the innovative capabilities of these immersive technologies. By incorporating a nuanced customer journey model, the paper elucidates how consumer interactions evolve within the context of extended reality and the Metaverse, thereby distinguishing these practices from traditional digital marketing paradigms.

The exploration of reality redefinition within the Metaverse highlights key concepts such as reduced reality, normal reality, and augmented reality, each playing a crucial role in how brands can engage consumers. As the Metaverse establishes itself as a significant marketing channel, the paper anticipates a shift in consumer experiences from traditional flat media to immersive, first-person interactions over the next five to ten years. It discusses the implications of utilizing innovative marketing techniques such as Virtual Product Placements (VPPs) and Virtual Spokespeople (VSPs), which can enhance consumer engagement but also raise ethical concerns regarding potential misuse in predatory advertising practices. This underscores the urgent need for consumer protection measures in this rapidly evolving landscape.

The significance of extended reality technology in addressing the challenges of an oversaturated market is also emphasized, particularly for startup businesses, where practical implementation remains limited despite a growing interest in extended reality. The integration of extended reality into marketing strategies is positioned as a vital tool for enhancing customer experiences and promoting sustainable purchasing behaviors. By providing organizations with a competitive advantage, AR fosters greater brand acceptance and engagement across multiple platforms, including social media.

[1]Jagan Institute of Management Studies, New Delhi, India. E-mail: lakshaygupta1990@gmail.com
[2]Jagan Institute of Management Studies, New Delhi, India. E-mail: rk.singh@jimsindia.org
[3]Jagan Institute of Management Studies, New Delhi, India. E-mail: monikaagg85@gmail.com

Methodologically, the paper outlines essential steps for implementing AR in marketing, demonstrated through the development of a mobile application designed to promote a specific product. This application serves as a case study, showcasing the potential of AR as a powerful marketing instrument while also acknowledging its inherent limitations. Furthermore, the paper discusses the broader implications of the Metaverse as an evolving landscape that converges various realities, offering numerous entrepreneurial opportunities across sectors such as digital marketing, advertising, gaming, education, and tourism. It suggests that this convergence can contribute to reducing social inequalities and revolutionizing traditional business practices.

The study ultimately aims to explore effective strategies for businesses to build their brands within the Metaverse while investigating the benefits and impacts of such brand-building efforts. By employing a desk research methodology, the study seeks to identify critical research areas concerning consumer behavior patterns in this novel virtual environment. It emphasizes the importance of developing new communication concepts and methodologies that enable brands to engage meaningfully with users in the Metaverse, thereby ensuring that they remain relevant and competitive in an increasingly immersive digital landscape.

Keywords: *Extended Reality, Metaverse, Marketing Innovation.*

Brand Engagement Through Augmented Reality and Extended Reality

Purvi Makwana[1]

Brand engagement via Augmented Reality (AR) and Extended Reality (XR) is causing a shift in the manner in which companies connect with their consumers. This shift is occurring as a result of the provision of experiences that are both immersive and interactive. As a result of the blurring of the line between the digital and physical worlds, brands are able to develop one-of-a-kind, customized content with the assistance of augmented reality and extended reality. This results in an increase in customer engagement and loyalty. Brands have the capacity to foster more deep emotional connections, boost awareness, and motivate active engagement via the use of entirely immersive experiences or the overlaying of virtual components onto real-world settings. These marketing strategies may be beneficial for the brands. Moreover, these technologies make it possible for customers to experience products in real time, which not only helps them to make better informed decisions but also raises the amount of enjoyment they experience. When considered as a whole, augmented reality and extended reality are powerful tools that have the potential to alter the manner in which a business communicates its story, create experiences that leaves a lasting impression, and drive consumer connection in unique ways.

Keywords: *Augmented Reality Interactivity, Consumer Brand Engagement, Brand Authenticity.*

[1]RTM Nagpur University, Nagpur, India. E-mail: purvimakwana11@gmail.com

The Role of Augmented Reality in Shaping Consumer Food Choices: Insights from Active Inference Theory

Vaishali Pandey[1], Vibhuti Tripathi[2] and Pooja Yadav[3]

Introduction: Globally, the food e-commerce market is projected to reach $1.89 trillion by 2029 (Statista, 2024). The upsurge in third-party aggregators like Swiggy, Zomato, and Uber Eats has further facilitated this growth. However, creating a compelling visualization of food items that facilitates consumers' imagination on an online food ordering platform is of utmost importance to marketers. Food images presented online, appear insufficient to replicate the sensory-rich experience of dining in a restaurant (Petit *et al.*, 2022; Biswas, 2019), posing a challenge for online retailers. Immersive visualization modes like three-dimensional (3D) and Augmented Reality (AR) are newly introduced product presentation formats (Xiao & Benbasat, 2011).

Despite the widespread proliferation of technologies in the food service industry, limited knowledge exists on how these sensory-rich visualization modes might influence consumption behavior (Abell *et al.*, 2024; Petit *et al.*, 2022). Studies indicate that the real-time interactivity and immersive experience of AR—through visuals by overlaying virtual products into the real world (Smink *et al.*, 2019)—can facilitate imagined eating for consumers (Petit *et al.*, 2022; Cornil & Chandon, 2016). The present study, thus, aims to understand the sensory-rich experience of AR on consumption behavior by addressing the central question:

"Does sensory-rich visualization mode of AR increase consumers' food cravings and their likelihood of ordering food online?"

The proposed underlying mechanism: The study builds on the theory of Active Inference (Friston, 2018) stating that—"perception is an active process", i.e., mental representations (internal perception of product) guide evaluation and choices, and are constantly updated through actions (of generating sensory feedback). It is assumed that

[1]Motilal Nehru National Institute of Technology Allahabad, Allahabad, India.
E-mail: vaishalii2206@gmail.com

[2]Motilal Nehru National Institute of Technology Allahabad, Allahabad, India.
E-mail: vibhuti@mnnit.ac.in

[3]Motilal Nehru National Institute of Technology Allahabad, Allahabad, India.
E-mail: poojayadav2699@gmail.com

the interactive features of AR through sensory (touch and visual) control give sensory feedback to update the mental representation of the product in the consumer's mind. This mental representation of product occurs as a result of reduction in mental intangibility existing in online environment (Heller *et al.*, 2019).

Research Methodology: The study employs an empirical approach with a between-subjects experimental design to investigate the role of sensory-rich AR (vs 2D image) in influencing consumption behavior. The data is collected through convenience sampling and analyzed using Smart PLS 4 for advanced statistical modeling, including Structural Equation Modeling (SEM) to test the hypothesized relationships.

Findings: Augmented Reality (AR) has emerged as an effective presentation medium for creating engaging and immersive online food representations compared to static images. The findings indicate that—AR significantly reduces mental intangibility, thereby facilitating consumers' ability to imagine food product experiences by enriching their mental interaction with it. These results align with the findings of Heller *et al.* (2019). Study reveals that enhanced mental simulation of the food experience intensifies consumers' food cravings and increases their likelihood of ordering food online.

Implications of the Study: The research contributes significantly to the burgeoning literature on Digital Sensory Marketing by shedding light on how sensory-enabling technologies, like AR, influence consumers' food consumption behavior. From the practical perspective, the findings will help marketers choose the right product presentation mode for enhancing the consumer's likelihood of ordering online.

Keywords: *Augmented Reality, Online Food Ordering, Food Craving, Digital Sensory Marketing, Active Inference Theory, Mental Simulations.*

Are Virtual Influencers for Real? An Industry Perspective and Future Research Agenda

Sudhir Pandey[1] and Bijal Mehta[2]

The trend of new digital marketing and social media technologies, such as virtual influencers (VIs), has grown recently, with various brands implementing these computer-generated figures into their strategies. Such VIs portray the human body and behaviours, interacting with users on multiple platforms such as Instagram and YouTube (Arsenyan & Mirowska, 2021). The increasing concern among marketers has been caused by the growing popularity of VIs and the issues surrounding their authenticity, ethics, and sustainability as marketing instruments.

Virtual influencers like Lil Miquela and Shudu have millions of followers and advocate branded partnerships with elite brands, including Louis Vuitton and Prada. What makes them stand out is how they create new ways of interacting with audiences by creating worlds where the borders of the real and the imaginary intertwine. It is believed that higher viewer engagement is associated with VIs rather than real influencers due to perfect image projection and coordination (Conti *et al.*, 2022). Nevertheless, marketers have recently reported growing scepticism regarding the increasing acceptance of VIs. A study points to the issue of authenticity, which seems to be quite crucial in traditional human influencers' performances (Stein *et al.*, 2022). Even though VIs allow better control over the message and remove unpredictable behaviour, they do not have the authenticity that human influencers can create with their audience over time (Moustakas *et al.*, 2020). Therefore, the overarching question is: How do industry professionals assess the credibility, ethical, and enduring value of virtual influencers compared with human influencers within the context of digital marketing strategies?

Keywords: *Influencers, Virtual, Social Media, Authenticity, Virtual Reality, Augmented Reality, Marketing, Digital Age, Para Social Relations.*

[1] Amrut Mody School of Management, Ahmedabad University, Ahmedabad, India.
E-mail: sudhir.pandey@ahduni.edu.in

[2] Amrut Mody School of Management, Ahmedabad University, Ahmedabad, India.
E-mail: bijal.nishant@gmail.com

[Submission ID 9275 • Track 8]

The Impact of Heatmap Metrics on Consumer Decision-Making in Metaverse Fashion Spaces

Reshmi Manna[1], Ankit Singh[2] and Kirtika Chetia[3]

A study using heat-map data on metaverse users' navigation and interaction with digital products aims to identify high-engagement zones for improved user satisfaction and retention. The research highlights the impact of metaverse virtual shopfronts on consumer engagement and purchases and the metaverse's sustainability and innovation discourse. The study suggests that brands should focus on engaging experiences, such as avatar customization or virtual fashion shows, and identify weeks and product categories with solid correlations to better time promotions to drive sales.

Keywords: *Metaverse Fashion Spaces, Heatmap Metrics, Consumer Decision-Making, Scroll Depth, Time Spent, Click.*

[1]Entrepreneurship Development Institute of India, Ahmedabad, India.
E-mail: dr.reshmi.manna@gmail.com

[2]Lintl Clothing Private Limited, Noida, India. E-mail: jaglan.ankit1207@gmail.com

[3]Entrepreneurship Development Institute of India, Ahmedabad, India.
E-mail: chhetiakirtika@gmail.com

[Submission ID 9865 • Track 8]

Unlocking the Power of Augmented Reality: How AR Boosts Consumer Engagement and Purchase Intentions in Beauty E-Commerce amid Perceived Risk

Archana Sarkar[1] and Gaurav Rajput[2]

Augmented Reality (AR) has emerged as a transformative tool in online retail, offering immersive shopping experiences that bridge the gap between physical stores and e-commerce. This study aims to explore the impact of Augmented Reality (AR) attributes such as virtual try-on, 3D product visualization, interactive tutorials, and personalized recommendations on consumer engagement and purchase intention in the beauty e-commerce sector. By applying the Stimulus- Organism- Response (S-O-R) model, this study examines the consumer engagement as mediator and perceived risk as moderator variable. Data were collected form 389 women respondents of Charotar region of Gujarat state who frequently shop beauty and cosmetics items from AR enabled platform such as Nykaa, Myntra, Amazon and Tira. Using validated scale, a structured questionnaire was developed. Python was used for data analysis by applying regression analysis and moderation-mediation analysis. Findings disclose that personalized recommendations and 3D product visualization significantly boost consumer engagement and purchase intentions aligning prior research that accentuate tailored and immersive experience. Yet, virtual-try-ons and interactive tutorials show mixed effects with potential disadvantages stanching from poor design or unrealistic outcomes. The moderating role of perceived risk conceded nuanced results, highlighting its influence under specific conditions. These findings propose that while advanced digital instruments can enrich experiences of consumers, their success heavily depends on refinement regarding virtual engagement strategies that best attains effectiveness and consumer trust.

Keywords: *Augmented Reality (AR), Consumer Engagement, Purchase Intentions, Perceived Risk.*

[1]Indukaka Ipcowala Institute of Management, Charotar University of Science and Technology (CHARUSAT), Anand, India. E-mail: archanasarkar.mba@charusat.ac.in

[2]Indukaka Ipcowala Institute of Management, Charotar University of Science and Technology (CHARUSAT), Anand, India. E-mail: gauravrajput.mba@charusat.ac.in

TRACK 9

Marketing and Sustainability

[Submission ID 2528 • Track 9]

Is Sustainability in Fast Fashion a Practice or Hoax? Analysing Zara and H&M's Sustainability Report through Impression Management Theory

Anupa Barik[1] and Neha Arora[2]

This research explores the intersection of fast fashion, sustainability, and corporate impression management. Fast fashion, characterised by rapid production and overconsumption cycles, poses significant environmental and ethical challenges. The study assesses how leading fast-fashion brands, Zara and H&M (Inditex), employ assertive impression management tactics to shape their public image and remove these challenges. Through a qualitative content analysis of sustainability reports, the research identifies key impression management strategies: Ingratiation, Self-Promotion, Exemplification, Supplication and Intimidation. While these strategies add to a positive brand perception, the study accentuates the need for genuine sustainability practices beyond mere PR practices. It focusses on the importance of addressing core issues like resource consumption, waste generation, and ethical supply chains. To achieve long-term sustainability, the fashion industry must prioritise circular economy principles, reduce reliance on harmful chemicals, and ensure fair labour practices. By critically examining the interplay between fast fashion, sustainability, and impression management, this research provides valuable insights for policy-makers, industry leaders, and consumers to drive valuable changes in the fashion industry.

Keywords: *Sustainability, Fast Fashion, Impression Management, Environment, Ethics, Greenwashing.*

[1]International School of Business and Media, Kolkata, India. E-mail: anupa.barik@isbmk.ac.in

[2]Dr. Vishwanath Karad MIT World Peace University, Pune, India.
E-mail: nehaaroradse@gmail.com

[Submission ID 3287 • Track 9]

Virtual *vs.* Human Influencers: The Role of Negative *vs.* Positive Message Framing on Environmental Activism and Sustainable Purchasing Purchases

Mehvish Marazi[1] and Tahir Wani[2]

The dawn of virtual influencers (VIs) has altered digital marketing. These avatars crafted through digital animation and AI have become prominent in promoting products, brands, and social causes on various social media platforms. While VIs has shown potential in engaging younger, tech-savvy audiences, the impact of their environmental advocacy on their actual sustainable purchasing decisions remains underexplored. To address this gap, we compare the effectiveness of VIs with human influencers in conveying environmental messages and fostering pro-environmental purchase behaviours.

The paper uses a 2x2 experimental design (virtual vs. human influencer) x (negative vs positive message frame) to examine how influencer type and message frame affect message effectiveness, environmental activism and sustainable product purchase intentions. Results show that a human influencer with negative message frames are most effective with respect to message effectiveness. Message effectiveness enhances environmental activism, knowledge and consequential awareness leading to sustainable purchases. Also, a multi-group analysis (MGA) revealed that environmental activism influences purchase intentions more for human influencers, while environmental knowledge has a greater effect for virtual influencers. The findings highlight the strategic value of human influencers with negative message framing in promoting sustainable behaviours.

Keywords: *Virtual Influencers, Human Influencers, Sustainable Purchase Intentions, Message Effectiveness, Environmental Activism.*

[1]National institute of technology, Srinagar, India. E-mail: mehvishmarazi93@gmail.com

[2]National institute of technology, Srinagar, India. E-mail: tahirwani@nitsri.net

Does Consumer Materialism Seriously Obstruct Pro-Environmental Behavior? A Systematic Literature Review

Linas Pupelis[1]**, Philipp Brüggemann**[2] **and Beata Seinauskiene**[1]

The increasing concern about climate change underscores the significance of self-interested values, such as materialism, which has historically driven economic growth. Hurst *et al.* (2013) conducted the first meta-analysis synthesizing research from 1992 to 2010 on the relationship between materialism and pro-environmental outcomes. In light of recent advancements in pro-environmental policies, there is a need to reexamine the role of materialism in relation to environmental considerations. A sample of 79 studies, reviewed using the 'Scientific Procedures and Rationales for Systematic Literature Reviews' (SPAR-4-SLR) approach, focuses on articles published between 2011 and 2022. While the majority of studies indicate a negative relationship between materialism and pro-environmental behavior, there is a growing body of research reporting non-significant or positive associations. This trend opens the door to new theoretical frameworks that explore the coexistence of these two seemingly contradictory behavioral orientations, suggesting that materialism may exhibit complex, multifaceted relationships with pro-environmental behavior.

Keywords: *Materialism, Pro-environmental Behavior, Sustainability, Consumer Behavior, Systematic Literature Review.*

[1]Kaunas University of Technology, School of Economics and Business.
E-mail: linas.pupelis@ktu.edu

[2]FernUniversität in Hagen, Germany. E-mail: philipp.brueggemann@fernuni-hagen.de

[3]Kaunas University of Technology, School of Economics and Business.
E-mail: beata.seinauskiene@ktu.lt

[Submission ID 5167 • Track 9]

The Impact of Sustainability-based Marketing on Consumer Buying Behaviour in Quick-commerce

Yashi Gupta[1], Shreejita Majumder[2], Yashasvi Shukla[3], Shaphali Gupta[4] and Rushabh Trivedi[5]

Quick commerce (q-commerce) platforms face the challenge of constantly optimizing convenience and speed to match growing customer expectations to achieve viability in a rapidly growing market. With a shift in consumer preferences towards sustainability within the retail sector, analyzing consumer attitudes toward sustainability in the q-commerce industry and its impact on customer engagement is crucial for businesses to thrive. The present study provides a conceptual framework that examines the extent to which consumers' attitudes toward sustainability lead to customer engagement through purchase intention, satisfaction, and positive emotions toward the firm's sustainability practices. This study also investigates how the consumer's awareness of the firm's sustainability-based marketing and the consumer's perceived effectiveness moderates the relationship between one's attitude towards sustainability and intention to purchase from the quick commerce platforms. The research reported opens future avenues for exploration into the impact of sustainable marketing practices on consumer behavior and engagement. By leveraging these insights, q-commerce platforms can develop tailored marketing strategies that resonate with distinct consumer segments. In-depth understanding of consumer behaviour with respect to sustainability can help firms strategize in the competitive marketplace. In conclusion, this study seeks to contribute to a more sustainable future for q-commerce by providing insights into effective marketing strategies and consumer preferences by identifying the value created by sustainable marketing initiatives for q-commerce businesses and consumers.

Keywords: *Sustainability, Quick Commerce, Sustainable Marketing, Consumer Behavior, Consumer Engagement.*

---

[1] MICA, Ahmedabad, India. E-mail: yashigupta.24@micamail.in

[2] MICA, Ahmedabad, India. E-mail: shreejitamajumder.24@micamail.in

[3] MICA, Ahmedabad, India. E-mail: yashasvishukla.24@micamail.in

[4] MICA, Ahmedabad, India. E-mail: shaphali.gupta@micamail.in

[5] MICA, Ahmedabad, India. E-mail: rushabh.trivedi@micamail.in

CSR Communication for Sustainable Branding: An Exploration through Stakeholder Lens

Anjali S. Menon[1], K. Rajasekharan Pillai[2] and P. Yogesh Pai[3]

Purpose: Sustainability branding has become a pressing need in today's dynamic business landscape. It is a concept closely linked with CSR and communication strategies. Stakeholders place greater emphasis on the sustainability and ethics of a company during the decision-making. The role of social media has amplified awareness and exploration of sustainability branding. This study unfolds how companies envisage sustainable branding through responsible communication initiatives and examines the outcomes and attributes perceived by stakeholders within the Indian corporate context.

Design/Method: This qualitative study employs a dual-method approach, combining exploratory content and thematic analyses. The sample includes Indian corporations awarded for their best CSR practices in 2022 by the Ministry of Corporate Affairs. The primary data collection was through Focus Group Discussions (FGDs) and secondary data from the online platforms of these corporations. A stimuli design, incorporating data from secondary sources such as social media platforms, websites, and relevant literature, was integrated into the interview guide. Online data were analysed using content analysis. And, the verbatims from the interview transcripts were subjected to thematic analysis to answer the focused research questions.

Findings: The findings reveal that sustainability branding is crucial for staying relevant in a constantly evolving market. Stakeholders increasingly favour brands that build meaningful connections and demonstrate consistency in their communication and actions. Companies have leveraged sustainability strategies and its applications with regards to both marketing and communication departments. Stakeholder posit the need for both company and the product to be sustainable in nature. Furthermore, the study found that stakeholders being more aware of these branding efforts expect clarity in the communication of actions, intent, and outcomes. Stakeholders also acknowledge that "sustainability" is a multifaceted term with various interpretations, requiring thoughtful and transparent communication and identify that incorporating

[1]Manipal Academy of Higher Education, Manipal, India. E-mail: anjalismenon96@gmail.com
[2] Manipal Academy of Higher Education, Manipal, India. E-mail: kr.pillai@manipal.edu
[3] Manipal Academy of Higher Education, Manipal, India. E-mail: yogesh.pai@manipal.edu

sustainability positions a company as a responsible brand. The insights from the study also sheds light on attributes created on stakeholders that affirm positive branding evaluations. These attributes also serve as key terms that are incorporated in communication threads.

Implications: This study offers insights for CSR and communication professionals aiming to design sustainable brands by comprehending stakeholder opinions and preferences. By deconstructing how stakeholders perceive different aspects of sustainability, the study helps professionals to understand and strategise content curation to create value, foster engagement, and strengthen stakeholder relationships.

Originality: The study highlights its novelty through both its methodology and sample selection. It is unique in examining the CSR communication of companies recognised by the government for their best CSR practices. Additionally, by conducting FGDs with an expert group, the study captured nuanced perceptions grounded in practical experience, providing valuable insights into emerging trends in sustainability and its interpretations by stakeholders.

Limitations: The study acknowledges the following limitations. The sample selected only Indian companies from a certain year, future researchers may incorporate a wider sample. Also, the participants for FGDs incorporated only expert group to garner in-depth understanding of practical strategies.

Keywords: *Sustainability Branding, CSR Communication, Stakeholder Perspective, India, Exploratory Design.*

[Submission ID 7207 • Track 9]

Perception of Generation Z towards Individual Social Responsibility (ISR) and Corporate Social Responsibility (CSR): A Communication Framework

Srushti Govilkar[1], Sarika Srivastava[2] and Ruchi Tewari[3]

Generation Z are those who are born between the late 1990s–2010s. As a generation it has witnessed technological boom. As the generation Z constitutes itself as one of the highest consumer demographics, and simultaneously entering the workforce, their perception of individual social responsibility (ISR) and how it views corporate social responsibility (CSR) becomes paramount given their inclination, awareness and active participation in the social and environmental concerns. Multiple studies are done from perspective of generation Z as the consumers and the impact of CSR of the firms' on their perception, brand loyalty, purchase intentions, willingness to pay, etc. The current study intends to understand the perception of the Generation Z on individual social responsibility (ISR) and corporate social responsibility (CSR) and explore commonalities to demonstrate their convergence to attract and retain them as employees and consumers. The method involved collecting primary data of 266 participants through a structured questionnaire based on a five-point Likert. The findings revealed that the Generation Z are quite vocal about social responsibilities both at an individual level (ISR) and at the institution level (CSR). The insights will help aid the corporates in strategizing, designing, and ameliorating their existing corporate social responsibility in a manner that caters to the generation by suggesting a communication framework which can help the organizations to have a comprehensive plan for the organizations to communicate with the Generation Z.

Keywords: *Generation Z, Corporate Social Responsibility, Individual Social Responsibility, Sustainability, Business Ethics.*

[1]MICA, Ahmedabad, India. E-mail: srushti.govilkar@micamail.in

[2]Graduate School of Management Studies, Gujarat Technological University, Ahmedabad, India. E-mail: ap2_cgbs@gtu.edu.in

[3]MICA, Ahmedabad, India. E-mail: ruchi.tewari@micamail.in

Greening the Fast Food Industry: A Hybrid Review of Sustainable Practices

Sumedha Rawat[1] and Shailesh Pandita[2]

The fast-food industry faces multiple pressures from environmental considerations alongside changing consumer preferences to switch over to more sustainable practices. This study analyzes 109 articles related to sustainability in the fast-food industry, using TCCM (Theory, Context, Characteristics, and Methodology) as the guiding theoretical framework. Theories such as Value-Belief-Norm Theory, Nutritional Footprint Theory, Theory of Planned Behavior, and Social Adaptation Theory were instrumental in providing insight into consumer motivation levels to join the efforts in promoting business sustainability. The papers collected community-investigated methods of investigating this topic, including mixed methods, quantitative, qualitative, case studies, and experimental designs. The assessments of each study were categorized into dependent, independent, moderator, and mediator variables, bringing clear perspectives on the interconnectedness of factors influencing sustainable practices.

The analysis points to key future trends and directions for additional research. These include technology innovations for alternative proteins, circular economy models focused on waste reduction, and energy-efficient operating systems. The research shows that context-based studies are much needed, particularly in developing countries, where sustainability challenges, comparisons, and contrasts differ from those in developed economies. Additionally, future studies should extend to longitudinal and experimental research to increase the understanding of how sustainability initiatives would impact consumer behavior and business performance over time. This review finds these gaps and new trends, which sets the stage for more research and proactive changes in the fast-food industry that will make it more sustainable.

Keywords: *Sustainable Practices, Fast Food, TCCM, SLR.*

---

[1]UPES, Dehradun, Dehradun, India. E-mail: sumedha.107541@stu.upes.ac.in

[2]UPES, Dehradun, Dehradun, India. E-mail: shailesh.pandita@ddn.upes.ac.in

Beyond the Purchase: A Sustainability Perspective on What Drives Today's Retail Shoppers

Sweta Thota[1], Naina Malani[2], Anna Vanduzer[3], Ka Wai Wong[4] and Adyasha Tripathy[5]

What is the influence of factors of (a) sustainability and social consciousness, (b) fast fashion and budget considerations, and (c) the pursuit of luxury goods on consumer choices for Gen Z and millennials? This exploratory research, through a mixed-method approach of survey research and in-depth interviews, attempts to provide valuable insights into consumer preferences, and shed light on the delicate balance between ethical considerations and traditional purchasing priorities in the apparel industry.

While findings indicate a widespread belief in the importance of sustainability, environment-friendly, and DE&I practices, quality, price, and style remain the top priorities for all generations, including Gen Z, when purchasing apparel. This highlights a complex balance: while consumers value ethical practices, they still prioritize tangible factors that directly impact their purchasing decisions, which contributes to the ongoing popularity of fast fashion.

This research also reveals that while shoppers are price sensitive, they justify spending more on luxury items for their high quality, unique designs, and versatility, in addition to the brand's prestige. This mindset positions luxury products as valuable additions to wardrobes, reinforcing the perception that they are worth the premium price, and allowing luxury brands to continue thriving. Managerial implications are derived from the findings of this mixed-method exploration. Continued research will be essential to keep pace with shifting consumer values and to refine strategies that resonate with diverse demographics.

Keywords: *Sustainability, Fast Fashion, Environment, DEI, Inclusivity, Social Consciousness.*

---

[1] University of San Francisco, San Fransisco, United States. E-mail: sweta.thota@gmail.com

[2] University of San Francisco, San Fransisco, United States. E-mail: nmmalani@dons.usfca.edu

[3] University of San Francisco, San Fransisco, United States. E-mail: alvanduzer@dons.usfca.edu

[4] University of San Francisco, San Fransisco, United States. E-mail: kwong50@dons.usfca.edu

[5] University of San Francisco, San Fransisco, United States. E-mail: atripathy2@dons.usfca.edu

Mindful Consumption in Digital Spaces: Exploring the Impact of Mindfulness on Consumer Responses to Influencer Marketing

Abhijeet Chitalkar[1] and Preetha Menon[2]

This paper addresses the theme and issues relating to mindfulness-based dynamics in the formation of consumer responses within digital spaces, such as resistance towards influencer marketing. With the rapid development of e-shopping platforms and online social media, new attention has been attracted with regards to the influence that these ultrasophisticated persuasive strategies have on consumer autonomy and decision-making. The study tests whether people who are more mindful are more likely to welcome a closer scrutiny of tailored ads and influencer posts, which would therefore result in more considerate and purposeful buying behaviors. Utilizing a mixed-method approach, combining both quantitative surveys and qualitative interviews, the study aims to measure the impact of mindfulness on consumer awareness, decision-making, and response to the strategies in digital marketing. Deepening the understanding of mindful consumption in digital spaces will offer practical implications for developing approaches to marketing that are suited to more conscious consumer values.

Keywords: *Mindfulness, Digital Spaces, E-commerce, Influencer Marketing.*

[1]FLAME University, Pune, India. E-mail: abhijeet.chitalkar@flame.edu.in

[2] FLAME University, Pune, India. E-mail: menonpreetha3@gmail.com

TRACK 10

Omni Channels and Retailing

[Submission ID 3747 • Track 10]

The Effectiveness of Omni-Channel Strategies on Sales Performance: A Meta-Analysis of Retail Case Studies in the Indian Market

Aditya Satbhaiya[1], Shivam Shekhar[2], Sashank Upadhyaya[3] and Chitralekha Kumar[4]

The impact of omni-channel tactics on sales performance in the Indian retail sector is investigated in this study. Omni-channel retailing has become crucial for businesses looking to combine physical storefronts with online platforms, mobile apps, and other digital touchpoints as a result of the retail industry's increasing digitization. The study's main objective is to assess the effects of omni-channel strategies on key performance indicators (KPIs), including revenue growth, client acquisition, retention, and operational efficiencies. The study also examines the difficulties Indian retailers encounter when putting these techniques into practice, especially in smaller locations, and provides information on how these tactics contribute to overall business performance in the country's quickly changing retail landscape. Using a meta-analysis methodology, the study compiles information from secondary sources, industry reports, and case studies. The case studies focus on well-known Indian merchants who have implemented omni-channel methods to improve their business operations, including Mamaearth, Nykaa, and Pepperfry. The study evaluates the effect of omni-channel strategies on sales performance, customer engagement, and operational efficiency by analyzing data from scholarly publications, market research reports, and financial records. While qualitative information from market surveys is utilized to evaluate consumer pleasure and experience, statistical tools such as regression analysis and correlation are used to investigate the relationship between omni-channel adoption and retail success. The results show that omni-channel tactics directly and favorably affect revenue and sales growth. For example, Nykaa has significantly increased sales

[1] Welingkar Institute of Management Development and Research, Mumbai, India. E-mail: adityasatbhaiya@gmail.com

[2] Welingkar Institute of Management Development and Research, Mumbai, India. E-mail: shekshiv1407@gmail.com

[3] Welingkar Institute of Management Development and Research, Mumbai, India. E-mail: sashankupadhyay733@gmail.com

[4] Welingkar Institute of Management Development and Research, Mumbai, India. E-mail: chitralekha.kumar@welingkar.org

by successfully integrating its e-commerce platform with its physical locations. The advantages of combining digital and physical retail touchpoints are illustrated by this success. By introducing offline kiosks, Mamaearth has also adopted a digital-first strategy that has greatly increased sales and clientele. These illustrations show how omni-channel retailing improves financial performance and generates more sales opportunities. Additionally, by providing a smooth and customized buying experience, omni-channel retailing increases customer engagement and retention. By offering individualized encounters through its online platform and physical experience centers, Pepperfry, for instance, has improved consumer loyalty. Through the integration of online and physical inventory, omni-channel solutions also improve operational efficiency. Businesses like Mamaearth and Nykaa have improved delivery times, decreased product shortages, and optimized supply chains, all of which have increased consumer happiness. However, the study points out a number of difficulties in putting omni-channel plans into practice, particularly in India's smaller cities and rural areas. These obstacles, which prevent retailers from growing their omni-channel operations outside of cities, include differences in digital literacy, logistical limitations, and uneven digital infrastructure. To sum up, omni-channel tactics are quite successful at boosting sales, enhancing customer satisfaction, and simplifying business processes in the Indian retail industry. Retailers must make investments in digital infrastructure and deal with the difficulties presented by India's varied retail environment if they want to fully benefit from these initiatives.

Keywords: *Meta-Analysis, Retail-Market, Omni-Channel, Operational-Efficiency, Revenue-Growth, Regression-Analysis, Logistical-Challenges.*

[Submission ID 7352 • Track 10]

Virtual Temptations and Impulsive Buying Behaviour in Retail Commerce: An Approach to Instant Buying

Riyaz Ahmed Qureshi[1], Aditi Srivastava[2] and Brij Mohan Singh[3]

This paper aims to study how virtual temptations affect impulsive buying on social platforms. The virtual temptations include three constructs - Social Influencer attractiveness (SIA), Content Appeal (CA), and Platform Reputation (PR). These elements influence Gen Z and develop a hedonic desire to buy restlessly without any interruptions in their buying orders. The paper is studying the mediating role of Social Influences namely- Informational influence (II) and Normative influence (NI). The relationship between Virtual Temptations (VT) and Impulsive Buying Behaviour (IBB) where Informational Influence and Normative Influence are mediators in the study. To carry out this research, purposive sampling is used in the study because only Gen Z is targeted for this study which is a frequent social media savvy user. The statistical tool used in the study is Structural Equation Modelling where parallel mediation is used to analyse the parallel effect of two moderators. A sample size of 300 respondents is being targeted via different platforms like LinkedIn, Facebook, Instagram, and WhatsApp. The tentative findings of the study will highlight the relationship between virtual temptations and impulsive buying amongst Gen Z and how effectively moderators –informational influence and Normative Influence drive more impulsive buying. This paper is significant in today's era where companies target Gen Z for low-budget products which can be bought impulsively.

Keywords: *Social Influence, Instant Purchases, Virtual Temptations, Impulsive Buying Behaviour.*

[1]Institute of Management & Research, MGM University, Aurangabad, Maharashtra, India. E-mail: dr.riyazsami@gmail.com

[2]ABES Business School, Ghaziabad, India. E-mail: aditisrivastava11@gmail.com

[3]Department of Tourism and Management, Indira Gandhi National Tribal University, Madhya Pradesh, India. E-mail: draditisrivastava11@gmail.com

TRACK 11

Services Marketing

[Submission ID 1910 • Track 11]

When Customers Cause Service Failures: Examining the Impact of Customer Behaviour on Service Employees

Rajani Balaji[1] and Shikha Karamchandani[2]

This study explores the critical role consumers play in shaping the outcome of service encounters, not only influencing their own experience but also impacting frontline staff and overall service quality. The interactions between consumers and service providers represent key "moments of truth" that significantly affect customer satisfaction, brand perception, and loyalty. The research focuses on understanding how consumer behavior, particularly challenging behaviors such as abusive or unreasonable demands, leads to emotional dissonance and exhaustion in service employees. As emotional exhaustion escalates, employees are more prone to negative emotional responses, which in turn increase the likelihood of service failures. The data will be collected from the service delivery employees using survey method. This paper aims to provide novel findings with many practical and theoretical implications.

Keywords: *Emotional Dissonance, Emotional Exhaustion, Negative Emotional Reactions, Service Failure.*

[1]RV University, Bangalore, India. E-mail: rajani.bali@gmail.com

[2]RV University, Bangalore, India. E-mail: karamchandanishikha8@gmail.com

[Submission ID 5316 • Track 11]

Exploring the Role of Organizational Commitment and Customer Incivility on Service Recovery Performance

Harshita Vyas[1] and Ashwini Awasthi[2]

Recognizing the critical role of front-line employees in maintaining service quality, this research aims to elaborate how organizational commitment can act as a buffer against the detrimental effects of customer incivility on service recovery performance. We have hypothesized that employees with high levels of organizational commitment are more resilient and effective in handling service recovery efforts, even when confronted with uncivil customer behavior.

The study is grounded in the conservation of resources theory, which states that individuals strive to obtain, retain, and protect their valuable resources. While high organizational commitment generally enhances service recovery efforts, the presence of frequent customer incivility can erode this positive effect by overwhelming employees' emotional and cognitive resources. Organizational commitment, as a critical resource, can mitigate the resource depletion caused by customer incivility, thereby improving service recovery performance.

Hypotheses are to be empirically tested with a survey of front-line employees from different service industries. The study would contribute to understanding how organizational commitment can buffer the adverse effects of incivil customer interactions on service performance. It would help practitioners to make appropriate interventions for improving organizational commitment of frontline service employees who face incivil customer behavior.

Keywords: *Customer Incivility, Organizational Commitment, Service Recovery Performance, Frontline Employees, Conservation of Resources Theory.*

[1]Nirma University, Ahmedabad, India. E-mail: harshita.vyas@nirmauni.ac.in

[2]Nirma University, Ahmedabad, India. E-mail: awasthiak@nirmauni.ac.in

Consumer Motivations, Knowledge, and Intentions: A Study on the Role of Innovativeness in Cloud Kitchen Adoption

Rishabh Mishra[1] and Madhvendra Misra[2]

The pursuit of new service models has revolutionized the food industry, with technological advancements giving rise to online food delivery (OFD) services. OFD platforms provide users with convenience, variety, and flexibility, allowing them to order from any restaurant (Wang *et al.*, 2021). The OFD industry has recently developed significantly through innovations and technology, notably with the emergence of cloud kitchens. Cloud kitchens are exclusive "kitchen-only" culinary concepts designed solely for delivery without dining areas (Jones *et al.*, 2024; Reiley, 2020) as an innovative concept, it is essential to investigate how consumer psychology affects motivations for adopting cloud kitchens.

Consumer innovativeness is a valuable predictor of engagement with new technologies (Vandecasteele & Geuens, 2010). According to consumer innovativeness theory, individuals with a higher propensity for innovation are frequently attracted to technological advancements and are likelier to adopt new technologies due to their inherent desire for uniqueness (Hwang *et al.*, 2019). It can be measured across four core dimensions driving consumer behavior: functional, hedonic, cognitive, and social. Previous research has examined consumer behavior in the online food delivery setting. However, a notable gap exists in understanding consumer behavior toward cloud kitchens as a newly introduced concept (Cai *et al.*, 2022), particularly from the perspective of consumer innovativeness theory.

This study focuses on functional (fMCI) and cognitive (cMCI), Functional motivation consumer innovativeness (fMCI) refers to innovativeness driven by innovations' functional performance (Kim *et al.*, 2019; Vandecasteele & Geuens, 2010). Consumers with high fMCI prioritize convenience, time efficiency, and accuracy when selecting new technology products or services (Ozturk *et al.*, 2016). In contrast, cognitive motivation consumer innovativeness (cMCI) is defined as innovativeness motivated by the need for mental stimulation (Vandecasteele & Geuens, 2010;

[1] IIIT Allahabad, India. E-mail: vngic.rishabh@gmail.com

[2] IIIT Allahabad, India. E-mail: madhvendra@iiita.ac.in

Ford & Nichols, 2019). Consequently, consumers with high cMCI are more likely to adopt new technologies after evaluating their advantages and disadvantages (Hwang *et al.*, 2019). The study aims to investigate how customers' motivations for innovation, viz. FMCI and CMCI affect their attitude and behavioral intention for cloud kitchens. Furthermore, the moderating effect of subjective knowledge on the association of functional and cognitive motivations with customer attitudes and behavioral intentions will also be examined.

Research Methodology: This study uses an empirical approach to investigate the effects of functional and cognitive motivation innovativeness on consumers' attitudes and behavioral intentions toward cloud kitchens. Data was collected using purposive sampling of adults aged 18-45 (Saunders *et al.*, 2009). The PLS-SEM approach (Lohmöller, 1989) was applied to assess the model and test hypotheses.

Findings: The findings highlight the significant influence of consumer innovativeness as a personality trait on the adoption of cloud kitchens, a newly introduced concept. Consumer innovativeness plays a pivotal role in shaping attitudes and behavioral intentions toward adopting this innovative platform. Furthermore, subjective knowledge significantly moderates the relationship between motivated consumer innovativeness and both attitudes and behavioral intentions, reinforcing its critical role in the adoption process.

Implication: This study contributes both theoretically and practically. It advances consumer psychology by exploring motivations for adopting innovative services and adds to cloud kitchen research. Practically, it helps cloud kitchen providers understand consumer expectations and how subjective knowledge influences behavioral intentions.

Keywords: *Cloud Kitchen, fMCI, cMCI, Subjective Knowledge, Behavioral Intention, Motivated Consumer Innovativeness.*

[Submission ID 8109 • Track 11]

Leveraging Servitization to Navigate Technological Disruptions in the Automotive Industry

S.S. Triveshika[1] and Shefali Srivastava[2]

The automotive sector is shifting significantly by implementing servitization strategies to navigate technological disruptions. The present study aims to know the current status of servitization research, its use in navigating disruptive technologies, and possible future research pertinent to the issue. The study employs BibExcel and Gephi bibliometric analysis to evaluate 479 articles retrieved from the SCOPUS database to estimate how the field of servitization evolved between 2020 and 2024. A network and descriptive content analysis were conducted to understand key drivers and barriers and provide a strategic framework. The findings shed light on the issues of integrating technology and putting dynamic capabilities into practice, although there have been significant developments in fields like sustainability and digital servitization. This study proposes six research themes, four spheres, and a division of servitization frameworks and functional dimensions to align business models with technological disruptions. The study concludes by outlining key implications and future developments in the servitization field that benefit academia and industry.

Keywords: *Servitization, Technological Disruptions, Automotive Industry, Bibliometric Analysis, Network Analysis, Descriptive Content Analysis.*

[1]Christ University, Bangalore, India. E-mail: triveshika.ss@res.christuniversity.in

[2]Christ University, Bangalore, India. E-mail: shefali.srivastava@christuniversity.in

Author Index